CHECK YOUR CHILD'S I.Q.

Other titles by Victor Serebriakoff in Sphere:

HOW INTELLIGENT ARE YOU?

Check Your Child's I.Q.

VICTOR SEREBRIAKOFF

**Test and tables by
DR STEVEN LANGER**

SPHERE BOOKS LIMITED
30/32 Gray's Inn Road, London WC1X 8JL

First published in Great Britain by Sphere Books Ltd 1979
Copyright © Victor Serebriakoff 1977
Test and tables copyright © Dr Steven Langer 1977

Set in V I P Century Schoolbook

Printed in Great Britain by
Hazell Watson & Viney Ltd
Aylesbury, Bucks

Contents

PART ONE

The Part You Must Read

CHAPTER ONE

Why You Should Want to Know

Let's settle one thing before we start. This book is about psychology and, in particular, psychometrics or mental measurement. The inquiring layman is bombarded with contradictory views that make him wonder whether he can be sure of anything in this field.

Now, if what you mean by *sure* is *absolutely sure*, then you should know right away that you will learn nothing in this book of which you can be absolutely sure. Psychology is just not like that. Yet. And it may never be.

In some areas of human knowledge, our information is so certain that we can discount the possibility of error. In most areas, however, the best we can do is to make an educated guess. For example, it is simple to measure accurately the exact size and weight of solid objects such as coal or sugar. Measurements of this sort are easily determined, and you can be sure of the results. But if you want to know the value of your house, you go to a professional to get an estimate. An expert's estimate is better than that of an untrained and inexperienced person, but it is still open to a chance of error.

Almost all the important decisions in life involve

3

judgements where information is uncertain, and it is not surprising, because easily settled decisions are usually obvious and do not need much consideration no matter how important they are.

Most parents want the best for their children as they grow up, and they have to make decisions that affect the children's lives. Among these decisions are what kind of education a child should have, when it should leave school, and what occupation or vocation it should pursue. These are some of the most important decisions parents will ever make concerning the future of their children. But the information available to parents when they make these important decisions is frequently inadequate. Consequently, the decisions are often far from the best.

The purpose of this book is to provide parents with better information that will help them to make better judgments and, ultimately, better decisions. The information is not – cannot be – certain. It will be, however, the best guess. You have every right to question it and to challenge it if it does not seem right, and you will learn how to do so most effectively.

It is more important than ever before for parents to have the information necessary to make the best judgements. Some authorities who might be expected to provide this information are reluctant to do so. Many psychologists, for instance, will not tell parents the results of intelligence and aptitude tests because they hold (wrongly, I believe) that parents cannot be trusted with this information. Teachers, doctors, and social workers as well, sometimes subscribe to the doctrine that 'we know best,' suggesting that they alone are equipped properly to interpret and use such test results.

It is principally this outlook that has persuaded us to make available an intelligence test designed specifically for the use of parents. This test is a 'first approximation' of I.Q. with normative data for children – the first, we believe, that has been made generally available to the public. In the past, the only widely available I.Q. tests have been those designed to test adults, and even of those, few have been subjected to the rigorous statistical examination that is necessary to make them truly predictive instruments.

We cannot really blame the psychologists or the teachers for their refusal to inform parents. They operate under a system of contradictory social, professional, and political pressures. It is fashionable to believe that the recognition of mental ability is anti-social and divisive. To select and recognize certain children as having good brain power, it is said, is at the same time to reject others. The 'rejected' children, the theory goes, are 'branded,' and their lower performance in the future is more a result of this 'labelling' than it is due to a basic lack of ability. We do not agree with these views, though they have gained wide acceptance. The intentions of the people who subscribe to these views may be honourable, but as a result, the concerned and educated parent who wants the best information available about his or her children may not be able to obtain it and so will be unable to set the best, most realistic education and vocational standards and aims for them.

The policy of nondisclosure goes even further. In many schools today, even the results of academic examinations are kept secret or are made available only on demand, lest the children be confronted with the 'horrible' truth that there are others who can better assimilate and articulate ideas. Often a teacher will carefully adjust reports provided to parents in such a way that every child appears to be of equal ability and promise. This deception denies parents the information they need upon which to base their judgments. They are left with only their own, sometimes biased, personal view of their children's abilities.

The publication of the tests contained in this book will not please the educators and psychologists described above. There will be many who will fear that the test may be misused, that parents are not sufficiently objective to test their own children, and that they would misinterpret the instructions and the results. Many others claim that this kind of test is meaningless. Let us look at the evidence.

We take the position that the overwhelming majority of parents who will be interested in this book will also be sufficiently responsible to use it properly and to interpret the results with common sense. Certainly, it is in their power to influence the result by bending the rules, allowing more time, or being overstrict. They will not be doing their children or themselves a service if they do any of these things.

We do not think that many will use this information foolishly or that the overall effect of publishing these tests will be harmful. Those parents who misuse the tests will do so to confirm opinions they already hold about the level of their children's intelligence. The worst that will happen is that they will have missed an opportunity to correct their views. The parents who really want to know fall into two classes: those, probably the majority, who have already made a reasonably accurate assessment of their child and those who may have incorrectly evaluated their children. Both groups will probably receive corrective information. Those whose views are confirmed will be able to proceed with confidence based on usable evidence and will be better able positively to direct and develop their children's future. It may surprise you when we say that it does not matter if you cheat and/or fail to follow the test instructions. You will be deceiving no one but yourself and such behaviour on your part tells a lot about both your attitudes and expectations. The parent or the person who undertakes to conduct these tests should be as careful, responsible, and serious as possible. Correct information will do the most good; wrong information will do no good at all. It is, therefore, of the utmost importance that you read all the instructions with great care, making sure that you understand them completely *before* you apply the tests.

We see a decline in the quality of the educational system, which may have been caused by ideologies influencing it, opposition to the idea of selection, or trends toward indiscriminate or so-called 'progressive' education. These factors have combined to increase the burden of responsibility the parent must carry. It takes as much courage to accept and cope with the truth as it does to seek the truth. For the sake of your children, you must not be dissuaded or discouraged in your pursuit of the best for them despite the fact that you will confront envy and a too-frequent conscious effort to stifle excellence and high-quality performance. Insist on knowing the facts about your children and do your best to see that this information is used in the most productive and beneficial way for them.

If your own perception of your child's intelligence is significantly different from the indication of this test, or if your child's score is very high or very low for its age, then it is most important that you do not rely totally on the test but let it stimulate you into seeking professional advice. With persistence you will find a psychologist who will test your children and give you not only the results but also a realistic evaluation and interpretation of them. Addresses where guidance may be sought are given on p. 148. Your local Mensa branch may help. For those readers unacquainted with Mensa, the following section will explain the function and aims of the society.

Mensa

Mensa is a unique society. It is basically a social club – but a club with a difference. Members have to qualify at the level of the top two per cent on an intelligence test. Mensa is proud of its diversity; its members come from all walks of life and have an astonishingly wide variety of interests and occupations. It is this protean aspect that enables Mensa's membership to reach across common barriers such as religion, race, ideology, politics, and social class.

Mensa's aims are extremely simple: social and intellectual contact between people all over the world; research on the opinions and attitudes of intelligent people; and the identification and fostering of human intelligence for the benefit of humanity. Mensa recruits its members by seeking out as objectively as possible those who are able to think for themselves.

Both authors of this book, Victor Serebriakoff and Dr Steven Langer, are Mensa members. Mr Serebriakoff has had much to do with the world-wide growth of the society, which boasts a membership of 35,000 located in over 60 countries. In many countries there is a network of local branches with a wide array of meetings and activities.

The British and International headquarters, from which a list of national addresses can be obtained, is located at *Bond House, St John's Square, Wolverhampton WV2 4AX, England.*

CHAPTER TWO

Intelligence: What Is It?

The great successes of modern science began when *exact measurement* was applied to human knowledge and understanding. When the predictions from a scientific theory were tested *numerically*, the accuracy of the theory could be checked and subsequently verified or disproven. That is why mathematics plays such a large part in modern science. And when exact measurement and mathematical methods were used, a new truth emerged. It was found that there was no such thing as exactness. Scientists could create a theory, be totally convinced of its truth, and then discover that the predictions arising from the theory tallied only approximately with the experimental results. Scientists had to be content with this. They also learned something else – to be very suspicious of *consistent* errors. Many important advances in science arose from the refusal of scientists to ignore consistent errors. Inconsistent errors, random errors – those that showed no signs of a trend or tendency – could be accepted and ignored. They were held to be meaningless. But repetitive, consistent errors often concealed errors in theory. Scientists began to develop a theory of errors, a set of mathematical rules that helped them to know what type and degree of error could be considered reasonably compatible with a theory and what sort of error would oblige them to abandon the theory. A later name for the theory of errors was *probability theory*. The new approach developed into an academic discipline known as *statistics*.

We should look upon statistics as the *measurement* of uncertainty – an attempt to assess in numerical terms *how* sure or unsure we are of something.

To give a practical example, we conduct our lives and plan our actions on the basis of certain expectations, beliefs, or *truths*. When we say it is *true* that the sun rises every morning, we base our belief on the fact that it has been found to do so regularly. But the truth of the statement 'the sun rises every morning' is valid only for some latitudes. At the North Pole or the South Pole the truth would be that the sun rises every year. For regions between the North and South Pole, the statement 'the sun rises every morning' would be only partly true. There are periods at midsummer and midwinter when it either fails to rise or fails to set. All these differences in the *truth* of the statement at different geographical locations lead, finally, to a much more exact and predictive theory by which sunrise and sunset at any place on the earth can be predicted with a great deal of accuracy.

In its simple way, this example shows the difference between prescientific truth and post-scientific, or numerical, truth. On the one hand, there is a flat simple statement: 'The sun rises every day'; on the other, there are a large number of seasonal sunrise and sunset tables for as many different intervals of latitude.

However, even these tables are not absolutely accurate, and the exact moment of sunrise will be found to depend on other, more local, factors, such as the relative height above sea level of the observer and the hills at his horizon. Nonetheless, the tables are accurate enough for all practical purposes, and that, it turns out, is the most that we can usefully achieve in any science or art.

Very often, when the purposes change, we need more accuracy so that as science develops, further theories are required.

You may be getting restless, asking what all this has to do with the science of mental measurement. Patience. It is vital that your understanding of this point is perfectly clear. Science shows us that we cannot expect to know all the facts. We are limited to making the best and most practical guesses.

Science and Accuracy

There are many definitions and conceptions of the purpose of that vast and expensive array of activities that come under the general heading *science*. A view that is sensible, if not orthodox, is that science is the pool of international organized knowledge about the world, nature, and ourselves that is available to mankind. It is, surprisingly, sometimes overlooked that the advantage of having such knowledge is that it gives us guidance in our behaviour, tells us what to do, and enables us to see what will happen as a result of our actions. Science is good because it is predictive. Furthermore, many scientists believe that only insofar as it is predictive can science be relied upon.

The sciences vary considerably in the reliability and the accuracy of their predictions. Astronomy, the science that enables us to predict tides and sunrise, is generally very accurate and reliable in its predictions. On the other hand, meteorology is primarily informed guesswork about the weather. The predictions are not always accurate or totally reliable. Nonetheless, we are distinctly better off *with* meteorologists than we would be *without* them. Their guesses are better than ours. We make fewer mistakes with them than we could unaided. All sciences lie on a continuum of accuracy and reliability, with the more numerical and predictive sciences, such as astronomy and chemistry, at one extreme and the less reliable, less predictive, less accurate ones, such as sociology, psychology, and economics, at the other.

The sciences have been arbitrarily divided into two categories: exact and inexact. Many exact scientists deny the status of true science to the inexact sciences. The science with which we are concerned – psychology – is admittedly one of the less exact. However, it remains preferable to be scientific rather than unscientific, so until we find something better, we must guide our behaviour, as it concerns the working of our own minds, by what we learn from psychology.

The specific branch of psychology with which we are concerned is *psychometry*, the science of mental measurement. Some people believe that it was only when the concept of exact measurement was introduced into the field of psychology that it disengaged itself from its place as a branch of philosophy and became a science.

But if any branch of psychology has a legitimate right to claim the status of science, it is psychometry. Though intelligence tests are 'debunked' with great regularity by physicists, chemists, astronomers, sociologists, and some ideological extremists, they remain an essential tool of educators, of clinical, counselling, and school psychologists, and especially of those who work with people who are mentally retarded. Despite the fact (which is frequently rediscovered with dramatic emphasis and publicity) that they are neither completely accurate nor completely reliable (like all other scientific knowledge), they continue to be an important source of information that can help psychologists and teachers to solve people's problems.

When compared to chemistry and physics, psychometry is not as reliable or accurate. But compared to other branches of psychology, psychometry is an excellent wellspring of usable data. If the choice is between psychometric measurement of intelligence and personality and subjective guesses with no measurement at all, then psychometry is more reliable, more predictive, and, consequently, fairer. It is assuredly less ambiguous or uncertain than other methods.

How Do We Measure Uncertainty?

There are two kinds of uncertainty: the uncertainty of a prediction, which is called *probability*, and the uncertainty of a relationship, which is called *correlation*. A correlation coefficient is a measure of the relationship between variables.

What are variables? The finite human brain, in its attempts to understand reality, is forced to simplify. Every single event and entity in the universe is unique, but it is convenient for us to think about each one as being in a *class*. A class is the name of the mental net in which we catch a large number of entities or events that are unique but similar to each other. For example, the class *human beings* embraces all the members of the human race. While each person is unique and individual, we can make a number of very useful, predictive laws and generalizations about people as a class. True, we falsify nature as soon as we classify, but the mind has a corrective technique. Having accepted that an entity is a member of a class *man*, we can then determine how he differs from other members of that class – taller or shorter, brown hair or white hair, fatter or thinner. Each of these ways of differing within a class is a variable, and of course there are a vast number of variables within the class *man*.

Many useful predictive laws or generalizations of science have arisen from the discovery that one variable changes in unison with another. For example, the heat given off by a wire varies in direct relation to the amount of electricity that passes through it. The relationship is very exact. In another case, however, the way in which one variable changes with another may be less exact. Two variables in human beings, lung cancer and cigarette smoking, are related. However, not everybody with lung cancer smokes, and not everybody who smokes get lung cancer; yet there is a definite relation between the two. This is an example of a much weaker relation or correlation. It is a measure of how much one variable tells us about the other one.

Correlations are measured by a number called a *coefficient*, on a scale from 0, which means there is no relationship, to either +1·0, which means there is a fixed positive relation between the two variables, or −1·0, which means that they are completely related but that their relationship is reversed. As one variable increases, the other variable always decreases. It does not matter what the actual value of the variables are; it is the *strength* of the relation between them that is measured by the correlation coefficient.

The concept of a correlation coefficient, which has proven extremely useful in many other sciences as well, was first developed in connection with intelligence testing by Sir Francis Galton in the 1880s and advanced by Professor C. E. Spearman in the early 1900s.

The theory behind intelligence testing is that among the many thousands of variables between people, there is a very important one that concerns the general ability to deal with information and to solve problems. Measuring this variable by use of the correlation coefficient scale is a useful and sensible way of differentiating between people. Evaluating human differences on a scale where the congenital idiot lies at one extreme and the genius at the other is helpful to the educator, manager, or parent. Most of you, from your own experience, are aware of these differences. You refer to one person as being intelligent, clever, perceptive, crafty, and wise and to another person

16

as being dull, thick, and unintelligent. The adjectives may change but the meaning is always clear. However, there are scientists who seriously deny intelligence as a real factor in the human personality at all. They claim that this particular variable is unpredictive and therefore not worth bothering with, believing the evaluations to be useless. However, in the absence of an equally workable alternative, psychometry remains the best register available to us.

There are many definitions of intelligence, and there is little agreement among scientists about them. It was the British scientist Sir Francis Galton who first conceived of the idea of *measuring* intelligence. Before his time the word *intelligence* had been used to mean *information*. For instance, the intelligence corps in the army is that part of the army concerned with getting information. But Galton used the word intelligence interchangeably with *general ability*. It was only gradually that the word came to be used in its modern sense. We do *not* use the word intelligence for abilities that are actually *skills* by which we use our bodies well and direct our movements accurately and precisely. We use the word intelligence in connection with the ability to store and deal with information. We do not mean simply good memory; rather, we are concerned with the way the material in our memory is used.

Intelligence is about information, and information is always encoded. We say that a person is intelligent if he has a good information store (memory); is good at integrating new information with the information already in store; is good at simplifying, condensing, and assimilating information to use it more efficiently; and is good at manipulating and dealing with information so as to produce solutions to problems. We have previously defined it elsewhere and repeat it here: 'Intelligence is the capacity in an entity (living thing or artifact) to *detect, encode, store, sort, and process signals generated in the universe and transduce them into an optimal output pattern of instructions.' Optimal* means giving the most advantageous results for the individual or group for which the intelligence is operating. More simply, intelligence is the process of using information for the advantage of individuals or systems.

The Normal Distribution of Intelligence

The intelligence variable is an uninterrupted continuum; it spans evenly from the congenital idiot at one end to the genius at the other with the successive levels merging imperceptibly into each other. There are no sharp dividing lines.

Before the nineteenth century began, an important mathematical discovery concerning variability between members of a class was made by the mathematician Karl Friedrich Gauss. He found there was an extraordinary but typical way in which some things, especially living things, varied from the average. You can take variables such as height and weight and measure these for any large sample of people, and the results will show a definite relation between the number of people with any size or weight and the difference of that weight or size from the average. This is so well established that we can tell quite precisely how many people of any given height or weight there

18

are in any population once we have taken measurements of an adequate sample. To illustrate this in terms of human intelligence, first imagine that we select at random a thousand children from the population. Then we test all their intelligence quotients (I.Q.s) and assign each of them a mark – 50 to one, 122 to another, 171 to a third, and so on.

Next we take them all to a field, select one child of each I.Q. score, and line them up side by side along one side of the field so that the child with the lowest I.Q. is to the left. The first child may have an I.Q. of 50. A child with an I.Q. of 51 is next, one with an I.Q. of 52 is next to the child with 51, and so on. At the extreme right will be that very bright child with an I.Q. perhaps as high as 175.

The remaining children are then asked to line up behind the child with the same score as their own so that you have a line of children with an I.Q. of 50, and then another line of children with an I.Q. of 51, then one with an I.Q. of 52, and so on. What Gauss's law tells us is that if we look down on the field from above, when all the children have been arranged in lines according to the numerical designation of their various I.Q.s, we will see that the shape of the crowd is that of the gaussian or bell curve as illustrated in the following graph. The lines will be the longest around an I.Q. of 100, which can be considered the average. As the lines of children move to the left and to the right of 100, we see fewer and fewer children in each line. As you get nearer to the extreme left or extreme right, the curve tails off until there is only an odd scattering of children in each line. The obvious conclusion is that there are very few extremely clever or extremely retarded children a long way from the average.

We would see exactly the same pattern, though with different children in each column, whether we measure height, weight, or any other similar variable. Gauss's discovery enables us to deal with a vast range of variables among large numbers of human beings.

One generally accepted theory of intelligence is that it is the external sign of an important underlying variable of the human personality that affects the ability or competence of a person to perform many different tasks. A very large number of trials on many different populations in all parts of the world have always led to a single, invariable result: there is a persistent correlation between different abilities in the same set of children. There is a clear tendency for children who do well at one task involving handling information to do well at all such tasks. If we divide any class of children into two groups according to their ability at arithmetic, and then do the same for English, geometry, history, drawing, algebra, physics, and chemistry, we shall find that the group that scores the highest in one subject will also be above average in every other subject.

For example, let us take English and arithmetic. Suppose that there is no association between the ability to perform well at these two tasks. We would expect to find that the top group in English would contain only about a half of the top group for arithmetic (and vice versa); but we never find this. Instead, we always find that the worst group in English contains *more than half* of those that

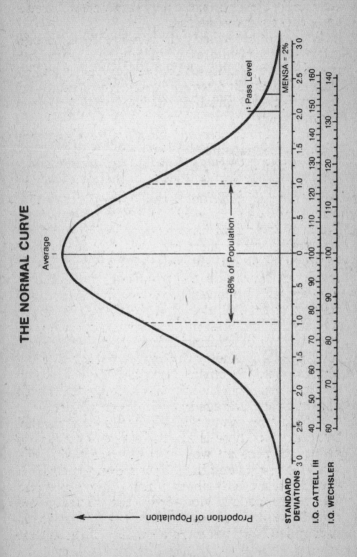

THE NORMAL CURVE

Average

68% of Population

Pass Level

MENSA = 2%

Proportion of Population

STANDARD DEVIATIONS	3.0	2.5	2.0	1.5	1.0	.5	0	.5	1.0	1.5	2.0	2.5	3.0
I.Q. CATTELL III	40		50		60	70	80	90	100	110	120	130	140	150	160
I.Q. WECHSLER	60		70		80		90	100	110	120	130	140

did worst in arithmetic, and the best group in English always contains more than its fair share of those who did best at arithmetic. Measured in terms of the correlation coefficient, the correlation is, not 0, but approximately 0·5, and this applies roughly, no matter what pair of subjects we use in the experiment. Contrary to the popular myth, there is no law of compensation that insures that those who are good at one thing are poor at another, and that those who lack in one field have a compensatory ability in another. The feeling that there is such a law of compensation is widespread and leads to the idea that the very intelligent child is skinny, puny, unhealthy, and unathletic. The view is based entirely on a sense of justice and not at all on facts. The facts are the reverse. Those children who distinguish themselves at schoolwork and who have a higher I.Q. turn out, on the whole, to be stronger, healthier, and taller and are able to run faster and play games better than the others. It may be unfair, but it is true.

It was the unexpected and unwelcome discovery that ability did not occur on a 'fair share' basis that forced the pioneers of intelligence testing, Sir Cyril Burt* and Professor C. E. Spearman, to formulate the concept of *general ability*, an all-round mental competence or efficiency that affects the ability of the person in any field to which he applies himself. General ability is the most important of human aptitudes. The ability to store and retrieve information, to form concepts, to see relationships and to make deductions from those relationships, and to assimilate material and formulate new combinations is what distinguishes humanity from the rest of animal life. It is to this general ability, this intelligence, that man owes his present pre-eminent position as master of the earth.

*An article in the London *Sunday Times*, October 1975, based on a book by Dr Oliver Gillie, made a number of sensational, serious charges against Professor Sir Cyril Burt.

Sir Cyril, who was Britain's outstanding psychologist for many years and who had been knighted for his services to education, had achieved world fame for his contributions, in the early days, to psychometrics, to social psychology, and to behavioural genetics.

Gillie's allegations were that Burt was guilty of 'scientific chicanery' and 'fraud' in his work. Gillie claimed that Burt had published articles in collaboration with two ladies whom Gillie said did not actually exist. He also claimed that Burt made estimates rather than actually measuring the I.Q.s of many of his subjects, and that there was a suspiciously exact correspondence between the correlation coefficients that Burt had published relating to samples of different sizes (a statistically almost impossible result).

Dr Oliver Gillie and a number of other psychologists, including Professor Rose of the British Open University, claimed that these charges must lead to the virtual abandonment of the view that heredity had any important part to play in the differences in manifest intelligence.

First, we must notice that this attack on Burt was conducted entirely in the columns of the popular press and not, as one would have thought necessary, in the appropriate scientific journals.

Those who supported Burt in the resulting controversy have pointed out that the doubts about some of Sir Cyril's pioneer work were first discovered and published in the scientific journals by Professor Arthur Jensen, who is well known to be a strong supporter of the hereditarian point of view.

Professor Jensen said that much of Burt's early work has now been shown not to have the rigour that would be required by the modern science of psychometrics, but since Burt's general conclusions are supported by more than one hundred similar independent inquiries that are not open to the same objections, Burt's conclusions are not seriously in doubt.

To the charges of 'scientific chicanery' and 'fraud' that Gillie brought against Burt, I should like to reply by quoting from a

23

January 1977 article in the British journal *Encounter*, by Professor H. J. Eysenck: 'Ideologised fanatics have always tried to expunge heresy to the best of their ability, without regard for facts, justice, or compassion. Hitherto, this has fortunately not been the climate of modern science. Jensen not only discovered the discrepancies in Burt's data; he also indicated in his article how such unfortunate occurrences could be avoided in the future. I found his critical treatment of Burt uncompromising, but fair; Gillie's strikes me as unspeakably mean and senselessly derogatory.'

Eysenck's views are supported by the fact that two of the research collaborators whom Gillie suggested Burt had 'invented' were subsequently found to have existed. He also points out that Burt was a pioneer working in a new field where data were scarce, and the faults in his work could with more charity be ascribed to carelessness, error, and failure of memory.

The use of such words as *fraud* and *chicanery* would justify the counteraccusation of 'character assassination.'

Having followed the controversy closely, I am quite sure that none of Burt's general conclusions are left in doubt in responsible scientific circles.

Much of Burt's work may, it is true, have to be subtracted from the great pool of evidence that has been built up. This was already done some years ago in responsible scientific circles long before the sensational charges by Gillie had been made.

Burt's reputation as a scientist has suffered a little, but his honour and integrity as a great man and a pioneer in his field remain, to sensible, fair-minded people, unaffected.

I had the privilege of knowing and corresponding with Sir Cyril for many years, and my personal impression is that the sensational charges against him are comically absurd.

CHAPTER THREE

How Do We Measure
Human Intelligence?

What the intelligence examiner is trying to measure is *general* ability, which cannot be measured by a test that applies only to one particular ability. We have to employ a number of different tests, each of which is directed to examine a special aspect of general ability, or use one test that investigates several abilities. There will be tests of the ability to manipulate numbers (arithmetical tests); verbal tests, which will be concerned with the ability to use words accurately and well; tests that will inquire into the ability to understand problems concerning shapes and forms; and tests that will measure the ability to make rational decisions based on deductions from given facts. The collection is called a *battery* of tests.

The whole battery of tests consists of a number of individual questions within each category. The final result is a summary that measures or indicates the subject's all-round ability across the entire spectrum of tests. The tests are normally arranged in a rising order of difficulty, the most difficult questions coming last. The object of a timed I.Q. test is to discriminate; so the most difficult questions should be such that no one can do them in the time allowed. If, for instance, the most intelligent 10 per cent of children could do the most difficult questions, then the test would not be discriminating among the top 10 per cent. No one should, therefore, be surprised if the child fails to finish the course. The child is either very careless or extraordinarily bright if he does – or there is something wrong with the test. The tests in this book are not *time* tests but what is known as *power* tests. On these, the child may take as long as he wants. All children should find these tests too difficult at some point.

There are two types of tests: open ended and closed ended. The open-ended test asks questions to which there can be a number of correct answers, for example, 'Name a mammal that lives in the sea.' 'Whale' or 'porpoise' are both good answers. Closed-ended tests have multiple choice questions that give a limited number of alternatives to select from, for example, 'Which of the following animals is a mammal and also lives only in the sea – walrus, porpoise, shark, or herring?' In this case, the only answer is 'porpoise,' as the others either are not mammals or spend some of the time out of the sea. The closed-ended question with a limited choice has an administrative advantage. It can be unambiguously marked by anyone with modest clerical skill. The marker does not need to understand the questions as they are marked from a key. Open-ended questions require interpretation and much more skill and intelligence in the marker. They also allow subjective judgment to affect the answer. Close-ended questions are more objective, provided they are properly composed and the accuracy of the answers has been thoroughly checked.

A distinct disadvantage of open-ended questions is that they create significant problems statistically. It is more difficult to measure the probability of, and therefore the implication of, a correct answer.

And it is necessary to remember that there is always a chance in a closed-ended test that the person will arrive at the correct answer by accident. In the example of a closed-ended question given above, there are four possible answers, so there is a one-in-four chance (a probability of 0·25) that the person may get the answer right by having selected it at random, arbitrarily. You have to accept the fact that an element of chance enters into any measurement of this type of test.

However, the probability that anyone would achieve a high score in a whole battery of closed-ended tests by chance is very low. The rule is simple. The probability of getting one item right if there are four alternatives is one in four; the probability of getting two items right is one in sixteen; the probability of getting three items right is one in sixty-four. The mathematical equation for calculating this probability is

$$p = \left(\frac{1}{x}\right)^n$$

where p = the probability of a chance explanation, x = no. of choices and n = no. of questions.

$$p = 0·25^3 \text{ (3 questions)}$$
$$p = 0·0156$$

The rule is multiply the probabilities. A test of twenty-five items with four alternatives each leaves a negligible probability (over a thousand billion to one) of a correct solution of all items by chance. However, there is a distinct and measurable possibility of getting a noticeably *better* score by chance, especially if the person follows the optimum strategy of guessing when the answer is not known. In most I.Q. tests there is usually no penalty for wrong answers.

Experience has shown that even when a person thinks he is making a wild guess, the answer is more affected by his intelligence than he realizes. Certainly, in the test that follows, you should encourage the child to make a guess if he or she is sure the answer will not come with a little more thought.

While the odds against succeeding by luck can be easily calculated with closed-ended tests, they cannot be so easily calculated with the open-ended ones. Obviously, when the test results are used to assess I.Q., an allowance is made for the chance or luck effect since this effect cannot be eliminated.

What other uncertainties are there in intelligence testing? Each test is applied to a sample (as large as possible) of the population in order to establish both the average score and the way in which groups of people deviate from the average. This is referred to as the *standard deviation* or *spread* of the distribution. It is a sign of a good intelligence test if this spread follows the pattern of the normal distribution curve, as in the graph on page 21. If the test is badly constructed, it will have a distorted curve, and the psychologists will know that something is wrong.

The next question of validity arises from the actual population that is used as a sample. Ideally, a random sample of the whole of humanity should be used to check the veracity of a test, but that is obviously impractical. Therefore, the psychologist has to do the best he can to obtain a widespread, random sample of people to establish an average so that anyone tested can be placed with respect to it.

The psychologist is usually forced to work with one language group in one country, so what he is actually determining is the average for that subdivision of humanity and the way that group deviates from the average. But there is very good reason to suspect that different groups within one country, even though they may speak the same language, are exposed to different ideas and concepts and therefore do not perform in the same way on any test. Sociologists and anthropologists speak of these different groups as classes, cultures, subcultures, or socioeconomic groups. Sometimes these different groups have the same average score and spread of scores as others, but more frequently there are marked differences between one group and another. While there is not so much difference in the spread of scores, usually the average score is different.

There are two very disparate views about these differences held by sociologists and psychologists, and there is a great deal of controversy on the subject. The issue is, that it is usually those groups that have less money and fewer privileges that, generally speaking, average lower on these tests. The upper and middle classes tend to have a higher average score, though they still have a wide spread just as the other socioeconomic groups do. Skilled workers have a medium score, while unskilled workers and underprivileged minorities are found to score, on the average, at a lower level. The difference in averages creates a controversy primarily because of its political implications. We do not intend to enter too deeply into this controversy; rather, we will simply state the different views.

One point of view, put forward by a group of psychologists, believes that the differences in the average score of the various groups reflect, or may reflect (most of them will admit that much more research needs to be done before we can be sure), real differences of average mental ability between various human groupings.

Mongolians such as Eskimos, Chinese, and Japanese, they say, have the highest average score. Caucasian whites, especially northern ones, come next on the scale. Mexicans and southern Europeans generally come slightly lower, and black people lower still.

Looking at social classes, they find that working class people in skilled occupations average higher scores than those who follow manual occupations, and clerical and professional workers come successively higher.

They believe that these scores may reflect significant innate differences. Those who hold these views do not speak of the entire class or group as being higher or lower but say that the group average is higher or lower. They point out that the spread of intelligence from the brightest to the dimmest in all the groups is still very great, much greater than the differences in the averages. From this it follows that race or skin colour is a very poor guide to intelligence.

The opposite point of view is that there is no

evidence to support the belief that there are any differences between the average intelligence of different ethnic and socioeconomic groups and that it is inadmissible to investigate the question because any test of intelligence must of necessity be biased against particular groups.

The principle upon which our test has been constructed is to use as many items as possible that have no content in language, because the language patterns of different groups are appreciably different and also because the test may be used in many countries. The test has been standardized on two groups of children in the vicinity of Chicago, U.S.A. These groups have been selected specifically in an attempt to span the spectrum of group average differences and socioeconomic bias. A discussion concerning the way the test in this book was developed by Dr Langer is given on page 47.

In choosing items not associated with language (nonverbal items), we have had to make a small sacrifice of accuracy since verbal tests seem to be a better aid in determining intelligence than other types of tests. The factor *general ability* seems to have more effect on success in verbal than in nonverbal tests. Therefore, a child who is good with words may be somewhat penalized. Those whose intelligence seems to favour their understanding of shapes and forms or reasoning will be somewhat advantaged. Parents can make some allowance for this in assessing the results. Professor Raymond Cattell, however, feels that these 'culture fair' tests are much better at detecting innate or genetic 'fluid ability.' He feels that verbal tests measure 'crystallized ability,' which is partly environmental.

Individual Tests and Group Tests

Experience has shown that carefully standardized individual tests give more reliable and consistent results than group tests; they are better predictors of later scholastic achievements; and, according to the experts, there is a much better chance of finding hidden talent with them. The disadvantages of a group test are obvious. With a large number of children being tested at the same time, it is not possible for the tester to observe individual differences in motivation or the various subtle signs that reveal that the test is inapplicable or unfair for that child. With individual questioning, there is every opportunity for a trained psychometrist to study the child, put it at its ease, and persuade it to do its best. However, this does not mean that group tests are of no use; it simply means that their reliability is somewhat lower than individual tests. It is not economically feasible for any school system to guarantee that every child shall occupy several hours of a highly trained specialist's time. The group tests, given the limitations of staff, time, and budget imposed by a school situation, are therefore the fairest and most practical method we have of assessing the child's ability and potential.

At this point, we would explain what the peculiar expression *I.Q.* or *intelligence quotient* means and how it arose. The first approach to measuring intelligence was to compare the score of individual children with a group average score. Of course, there was an allowance made for the age of the children. It was Alfred Binet, a French psychologist in the early 1900s and a pioneer of the intelligence test, who devised a test for determining the relative difference of the intelligence of children. The Binet test consisted of a series of questions and tasks graded with reference to the ability of the normal child to deal with them at successive age levels. It was administered to large samples of children of different age groups, and the average score at each age level was determined, the result being the so-called Binet scale. As the age of the children in the group went up, the average score improved. The score is simply the number of questions the child gets right. It has, at this stage, nothing to do with I.Q. and is called the raw score – it has not yet been digested and turned into a comparable score by allowing for age.

The average raw score for any age group is used to calculate what is called the mental age (MA). A bright child will score higher than the average for his age and probably will achieve a score equal to the average for some older age group. Let us say that the average raw score for the group whose ages are between six years nine months and seven years three months (average age seven years) is 162, and that the group whose average age is six years has an average score of 140. In practice, we know that quite a number of the children in the second group, the six year group, will achieve scores as high as and higher than those in the first group (the seven year group). Let us suppose that a child in the six year group gets the same score as the average of the seven year group: 162. Then we say that he has a mental age (MA) of seven although he is only six. Since we need another name for his true age, the choice of the psychologists is chronological age (CA). The great discovery of Alfred Binet, confirmed by many other psychologists, is that the relationship between the mental age and the chronological age remains surprisingly constant. The usual method is to divide one by the other, then multiply by 100 to avoid needing decimals:

$$\frac{MA \times 100}{CA} = \text{intelligence quotient (I.Q.)}$$

Using the above case as an example:

$$I.Q. = \frac{7 \times 100}{6} = 117 \text{ approximately.}$$

The intelligence quotient is a measure of the relation between the mental age and the chronological age for any child.

But this method of formalizing the differences applies only to children. So how do we deal with adults? The psychologists who were investigating the problem at the turn of the century soon discovered that while children always tended to get higher raw scores as they grew older, adults did not. In fact, there is even a slight downward trend in average raw scores between the ages of about fifteen and seventy years. After seventy, the decline is more rapid. The critical age, the age when the score stops improving, is usually fifteen years. In certain cases, where the I.Q. is exceptionally high, the raw score goes on improving for some time after the age of fifteen is reached. Improvements *can* continue until eighteen years old.

Therefore, you may ask, how can we speak about the intelligence quotient of an adult? As chronological age continues to rise, the fraction

$$\frac{MA}{CA}$$

declines since the mental age does not rise above fourteen to eighteen. The solution is simple. The chronological age for the purpose of I.Q. tests is given a cutoff point at some age between fourteen and eighteen (depending on the specific test), so the chronological age is not really the true age but becomes, for example, the true age or fifteen, whichever is less. With this provision, I.Q. calculations give consistent results that correspond with observed facts.

In the test that follows, we will show how to estimate the raw score of your child, how to apply the age correction and therefore read off the percentile rating and the intelligence quotient relating your child to the standardization group. (Parents who want to check the results they obtain or who need psychological advice should consult the British Psychological Society, 18 Albemarle St, London W.1.)

You may now be asking another question. If we determine the average for every age group to find the various mental ages, we reach a ceiling around the age of fourteen or fifteen. When people get to this chronological age the result of the equation

$$\frac{MA}{CA} = I.Q.$$

will tend toward 100 because there is no higher mental age than fifteen and the chronological age gradually climbs up toward this and then stabilizes. Confronted with this dilemma, constructors of the I.Q. test used another ad hoc solution. Very bright fifteen year olds had much higher raw scores than any other age group. It was simply that there was no age group that had an *average* above a certain level. However, by using the higher raw scores, the constructors were able to extend the range of mental ages by taking successive intervals of raw score similar to the intervals between the averages for the ages up to fifteen. These mental ages, or mental superages, contradict the other addition to the theory. As a result, testers say, 'mental ages do not extend beyond fifteen,' and then, 'but in a way they do.'

Confusing? Contradictory? It would seem so, but nonetheless the set of concepts and theories does lead to a reasonably predictive system. In our view, these concepts are of historical rather than practical value, and they are of no real importance to the basic theory. We have not come to the end of the deficiencies of the I.Q. measure of intelligence. The system is designed so that there should be no disagreement about the average score, which is contrived to coincide with 100. If all tests had been constructed in the same way, then the same group should have the same spread or distribution on either side of the average – that is, on all different tests, the number of people with a score of 105 should be the same as the number with 95, and the number of people with 120 should be the same as the number with 80. But it is not true. Different tests have different spreads or standard deviations, so that while I.Q. 100 is the same for all tests, I.Q. 120 means a different level on one test than it does on another. This is illustrated by the diagram showing how the scores on one test can be made equivalent to the scores on another.

In our view, it would do no great harm if the expressions MA, CA, and I.Q. were replaced with a set of concepts that were better thought out. These old expressions are part of the lore and mystery of psychometry, which, since they take a bit of understanding, help to preserve it as the realm of experts. They add little enlightenment and much confusion.

Fortunately, there is a much better way of doing the job that this set of concepts was set up to do. The base material of a completed, normed, and standardized I.Q. test is the raw scores of a random population of various age groups. From this data, we can calculate the average and the spread (standard deviation) in raw score for every age group, and from this information, we can calculate for every age group a simple figure called the percentile rating of any score for any age. The percentile rating can easily be illustrated in a table, and this table will explain, in a simple and comprehensible way, the only thing that an intelligence test can tell us – where an individual stands in relation to the rest of the population tested.

If you were told that your I.Q. was 160, you would have to acquire a good deal of experience to know exactly what that means, or you would need to know the standard deviation of the test. But if you were told that your intelligence was such that you were in the top 10 per cent or the top 60 per cent of the population, you could appreciate the significance of the remark immediately. That is the way a percentile rating works.

If a child falls just within the top 5 per cent, we say he 'falls on the 95th percentile.' If he is just in the top 10 per cent, he 'falls on the 90th percentile.' The idea is simple; the population is divided into one hundred parts, and the scores that would create such separations are calculated statistically from the known characteristics of the normal curve.

The percentile rating is a much simpler and more comprehensible system of expressing the classification of people by intelligence than the confusing and largely historical expressions explained above.

Regression to the Mean

One way of checking the reliability of intelligence tests is to give the same tests to the same group after an interval sufficiently long to insure that the subjects have forgotten the answers. Most people on retesting score within a few points of their initial score on a well-constructed test. Responsible test constructors will not accept a test as being valid unless the test-retest reliability, as it is called, is fairly high. However, looking at the results of these retests statistically, a trend emerges that ought to be mentioned. There is a persistent tendency for the lower scorers to get slightly better scores on retesting and for the higher scorers to get slightly worse ones, while those around the average have no specific tendency, some going higher and some going lower.

There is an element of chance in all results. Test

constructors try to control it and keep it as low as possible, but it is always there.

The more a score deviates from the average, the greater the probability that chance has contributed to the deviation – that is, if you take a group of very high scorers, you are likely to get more people whom chance favoured rather than opposed. Similarly, with very low scorers, there will be more who were unlucky than who were lucky. Given a second chance, you cannot expect the luck to be repeated in every case, so there will be a slight tendency for all scores to cluster closer toward the average next time. The more they do, the more part chance played in the result, but since the effect is not major, we can assume that chance played only a small part.

Practice Effect

Can children be trained to do better at intelligence tests? Yes, but only to a limited extent if the test is well constructed.

Professor Vernon, who investigated this question, finds practice will improve the score gradually up to 6 or 7 I.Q. points, but after that it levels off and no further improvement occurs.

The entire principle upon which intelligence tests are based is that every child should be confronting unfamiliar material for the first time. Each should be given exactly and precisely the same instructions so that everybody starts at the same level. Each time the test is given, a conscious effort must be made to reproduce exactly the same standard conditions of testing, as far as these can be achieved. But, of course, many children do not get second tests.

A solution proposed by Professor Eysenck to the problem is that all children should be given a certain amount of practice so that the practice effect can be absorbed and disposed of. However, if the original tests were standardized on an unpractised population, as they usually were, then the standardization will be thrown out by this procedure, and all practiced children will achieve slightly better scores than they should.

Nonetheless, within the normal accuracy of intelligence testing, we do not think this effect is of much importance.

Are Tests Much Affected by the Subject's State of Health?

A good deal of research has been done on this subject, and in a considerable number of experiments it has been shown that minor disabilities, such as headaches, coughs, and colds, make very little significant difference in the test score despite the fact that the subjects often feel they have not performed at their best level.

In the test that follows, it is certainly recommended that you should choose a time when your children are in good health. You are likely to have a better choice in timing than teachers or psychologists have, especially when they have to test large numbers of children within a short time.

Does a Child's I.Q. Change as It Grows Older?

The underlying hypothesis of intelligence testing is that I.Q. tends to remain the same relative to their age group as children grow older. While this is generally true, there are exceptions.

The correlation between I.Q. at two years and at eighteen years is less than 0·4, while between eight and eighteen years, it is above 0·8. After the age of ten, it reaches the limits imposed by the reliability of the test itself and is about 0·9. These correlation coefficients cover changes, which may be as high as 30 points or more, over the school years in individual children. Such large changes are uncommon. In fact, fewer than 10 per cent of the children will change by as much as this. However, changes of 1 to 10 points are commonplace, and around 70 per cent of the children tested will come within this range. Part of this fluctuation is accounted for by test error, though some of it is due to actual spurts and delays in the development of the children. Children from educationally advanced environments show a statistical bias toward a gain in I.Q., as do children from backgrounds where they started off with a higher I.Q. Boys appear to gain in I.Q. more frequently than girls, and, in fact, an advance in I.Q. is noticeably more prevalent in aggressive middle class males.

And What If the Children Are Not Trying?

It goes without saying that any test of a competitive nature is only applicable, valid, and reliable if the people being tested are really trying. A perfectly legitimate argument against tests under standardized conditions at school or at a clinic is that some children are not motivated to do their best either through individual inattention or because of preconditioned environmental factors.

If you suspect that your child is not trying, wait for a better occasion to administer the test, or the results may be meaningless. Parents know their children pretty well, certainly much better than teachers or psychologists do, so you will know when they are trying and when they are not. The kind of spirit to encourage is the competitive spirit of a game. They should not take the test too seriously and become worried or anxious about it. Nonetheless, they should certainly go at it energetically, with enthusiasm and excitement at the prospect of pushing themselves to their own limits. We believe that one of the advantages of parental testing will be in just this area. Most children will trust their parents and do more for them than they will do for teachers or strangers, however skilled and well trained.

CHAPTER FOUR

Giving the Test

The place where you test your child should be quiet, well lighted, and well ventilated. Just you and your child should be in the room; there should be no interference from or comments by other children.

Your child should have a pencil and paper in case he or she wishes to calculate anything before giving you an answer. You also should have a pencil. When your child makes its final decision as to the answer it wishes to give and indicates that answer to you, circle the picture or number your child has chosen.

The total uninterrupted time you should allow to administer this test should be between twenty and fifty minutes, including the time it takes for you to give directions to your child. However, remember this is not a timed test, so it is only a suggested time period, not a rigid limit; take additional time if necessary. It is important that you do *not* rush your child or make him or her anxious about a time limitation, especially if he or she needs encouragement to finish the questions.

It is essential that the child understand the directions before beginning the questions. A certain amount of flexibility in giving directions is permissible. You will know best how to be sure your child understands the directions without giving clues to the answers. The directions may be repeated as often as necessary, with *minor* variations each time. Use your judgment to decide when your child understands what is required and is ready to begin.

If your child has not yet reached the age of ten years and six months, have him or her answer *only* questions 1 through 43.

If your child is at least ten years and six months old, but under fourteen years and six months old have him or her answer questions 11 through 53.

If your child is fourteen years and six months old or older, have him or her answer *only* questions 16 through 55.

Some children do not take tests well and become easily discouraged and distracted. Therefore, if necessary, you should encourage your child to attempt to answer each question. Do not, however, pressure the child by belabouring any one question too long. If the child feels that a question is too hard for him or her to answer, pass it by temporarily until the child has attempted to answer all the questions for his or her age. Then return to any questions the child has not answered as yet. If the child cannot answer all the questions for his or her age, encourage your child to guess.

First, you should explain to the child that this is an interesting quiz, like a game, but that your child should try hard to see how well he or she can do. It is important to eliminate any sense of anxiety. You may need to take some time to build up interest and insure positive motivation. Be very patient and very encouraging. Be careful not to give the slightest clue to the answer by expression, word, or sound. Do not answer questions aimed at getting your opinion or give answers that would influence your child's decision in choosing its answer. Just repeat the question. The child is allowed only one choice among the answers given for each question. Reassure the child by telling it to take its time in studying the question so it will have confidence in its answer.

Your child will undoubtedly give a number of wrong answers. Accept them without comment. Do *not* ask the child any questions such as, 'Are you sure that's the right answer?' However, if the child *volunteers* that he or she thinks an answer may be wrong, encourage him or her to think about it a moment longer and then decide whether he or she feels it's right or wrong. Thereafter, accept the child's decision as to what the correct answer is, and mark the test accordingly.

The Test

When you are sure the child is ready to begin, start the test by reading aloud the test instructions.

After the child decides, circle the letter he or she indicates as the answer he or she has chosen.

Table 1 If the child is between six and a half years and less than ten and a half years

Table 2 If the child is between ten and a half years and fourteen and a half years

Table 3 If the child is over fourteen and a half years

On the appropriate table, locate the row corresponding to your child's age when tested. Using your child's raw score (the number of correct answers), go across the row from left to right, stopping at the number just equal to or nearest below your child's raw score. At the *bottom* of that column, you will see your child's approximate percentile rating on this test. This rating represents your child's position in relation to the standardization group.

The percentile rating figure represents the percentage of the standardization sample that *scored lower* than your child. For example, the 2 at the bottom of the column means that only 2 per cent of the children would score lower; the 98 at the bottom of the column means that 98 per cent scored lower, or only 2 per cent scored as well or better. The 98th percentile is the level of acceptance for Mensa, an international organization admission to which is based on performance on tests comparable to the one you have just given your child. If your child is placed in the 98th percentile, he or she would probably qualify for membership.

At the *very bottom* of the column that has the number just equal to or nearest below your child's raw score, you will see a number that represents an approximation of the I.Q. score for your child.

If the percentile achieved is very high, very low, or considerably different from your estimation of your child's intelligence, you would be well advised to seek professional testing for your child. A list of sources that provide information concerning professional testing appears in the Appendix.

We hope that you now have a better idea of your

child's potential and capacity and that you will use your knowledge for the benefit of your child, your family, and society in general.

How This Test Was Developed

Over a period of time, an item bank was developed of nonverbal items specifically designed to test the ability of children to recognize similarities and differences, to determine mathematical progressions, and to deal with quantities and spatial relationships.

Subsequently, these items were arranged judgmentally by order of difficulty, and a preliminary test was prepared.

Since it was designed to be a power test (testing a person's ability to answer questions regardless of the amount of time spent in the process), and since the time allotted for taking the test had to be limited to the time available during a normal classroom period, the test was administered initially to a small group of first and second graders to determine how many items we could reasonably expect all (or almost all) students in the lower grades to complete within a classroom period.

Thereafter, a subtest was developed that consisted of questions selected in ascending order of assumed difficulty and limited to the maximum number of items that could be completed during one period. This subtest was administered to the first four grades of elementary school (roughly ages six to ten). The results were analysed item by item and nonpredictive items were either eliminated or revised.

The final group of questions was rearranged by order of difficulty based on the analysis of the results of the subtest. The least difficult items were set aside temporarily, and the next, more difficult group of items was added to the original test. It then became a second, more difficult subtest, which was administered to grades five to eight (roughly ages ten to fourteen). The results from the second subtest were analysed as they were for the first subtest. Again, nonpredictive items were either eliminated or revised. A third, even more difficult subtest was then created.

The same procedure was followed with high school students, using the third subtest. After the results of the third subtest were analysed and refined, a fourth subtest was administered to a group of Mensa members so that those items that discriminated *against* individuals with high I.Q.s could be identified and eliminated.

When the item analysis phase of the study was completed, the first two (overlapping) subtests were administered to all the students in an elementary school (grades one to eight) with over nine hundred students in a middle class and upper working class area. The third, and most difficult, subtest was administered to three classes in each school grade in each of three different high schools. The classes were selected so that, for each grade in each school, one class represented a high achievement group, one an average achievement group, and one a low achievement group.

The test was developed in Illinois, with the assistance and cooperation of Mr William E. Augustus, superintendent of schools, Thornton Township High School District No. 205; Dr Harold

C. Scholle, superintendent of schools, Elmwood Park Community Unit School District No. 401; Mr John L. Corwin, principal, Elm School; Mr Ronald Habish, principal, Elmwood School; Mr Raymond R. Libner, principal, Elmwood Park High School; Mr Robert L. Littlehale, principal, John Mills School; Dr Robert A. McKanna, principal, Thornridge High School; Dr Robert C. Mitchell, principal, Thornwood High School; Mr John H. Smith, principal, Thornton High School; and their respective staffs and students. Without their assistance and cooperation, the development of this test would not have been possible. Our thanks are due and gratefully rendered.

To 'test the test,' it was administered to a group of high school students who were classified as mentally retarded. In view of this, the lowest level subtest (questions 1 to 43 of the test appearing in this book) was administered. The mean (average) score of this high school group was 23·1, approximately equal to the median for children eight years of age through eight years and nine months of age.

To 'test the test' further, the highest level subtest (questions 16 to 55 of the test appearing in this book) was administered to a group of Mensa members. The mean (average) score of this group was 30·4, equivalent to the 98th percentile of the oldest age group of high school students tested.

The mentally retarded students tested were not included in the normative sample since their scores would tend to make the percentile figures a little bit low. However, since the normative data were obtained in a group testing situation and you are administering the test on a one-to-one basis, this will compensate for what would otherwise be a minor discrepancy.

"In each of the following questions, there will be five pictures or drawings. *Four* of the pictures or drawings *go together in some way* or are the same in some way. *One* of the pictures or drawings *does not go with the other four* — it is different in some way."

(1) ● "*Which one* of the five drawings in Question 1 *does not go with the other four?*"

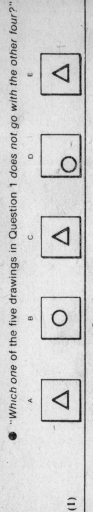

A   B   C   D   E

When your child has answered Question 1, ask:

(2) ● "*Which one* of the five drawings in Question 2 does *not* go with the other four?"

A   B   C   D   E

Now say: ● "*Which one* of *these* does *not* go with the other four?"

A   B   C   D   E

(3)

Then say: "And which of *these*?"
before each question through Question 15.

A	B	C	D	E

(4)

(5)

(6)

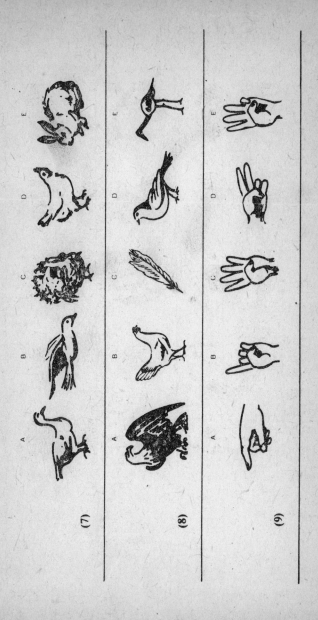

A   B   C   D   E   (7)

A   B   C   D   E   (8)

A   B   C   D   E   (9)

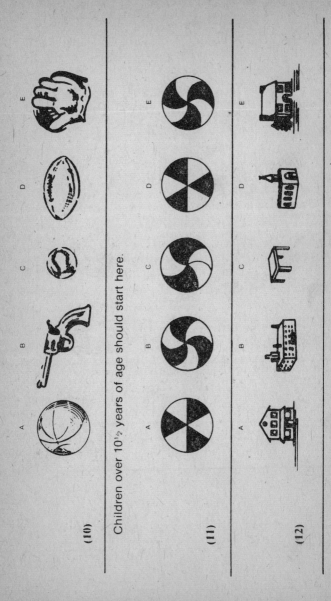

Children over 10½ years of age should start here.

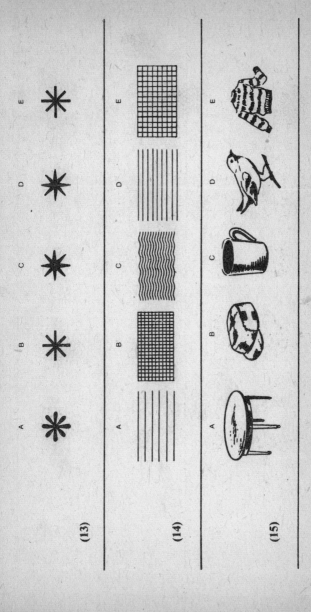

Children over 14½ years of age should start here.

Before Question 16, say:

● "Here is a picture of some blocks. How many blocks are there in this picture?"

	A	B	C	D	E
	1	2	3	4	5

(16)

Before Question 17, say:

● "Here is another picture of some blocks. In this picture, there are two layers of blocks. How many blocks are there in this picture? Remember that the blocks in the top layer have to have a block under each of them."

	A	B	C	D	E
	6	8	9	10	11

(17)

Before Question 18, say:

● "In this question, there are five numbers. The numbers are all getting larger. *Four* of them *get larger* according to some *rule* or *plan* or *pattern*. However, there is one *extra* number that does *not* fit the rule. Which one does *not* fit the rule?"

	A	B	C	D	E
(18)	2	4	6	8	9

Before Question 19, say:

● "This question is like the last question. However, here the numbers are becoming *smaller* according to some *rule* or *plan* or *pattern*. Which *one* extra number does *not* fit the rule?"

	A	B	C	D	E
(19)	14	12	11	10	8

Before Question 20 and up to and including Question 24, it is not necessary to repeat the complete instructions. Just say:

● "And how about these numbers?"

	A	B	C	D	E
(20)	10	12	15	20	25
(21)	27	23	19	15	12

	A	B	C	D	E
(22)	15	30	45	60	65
(23)	12	9	6	4	3
(24)	3	9	27	55	81

Before Question 25, say:

"The following questions are like some that you've already done. In each of the following questions, there will be five pictures or drawings. *Four* of the pictures or drawings go together *in some way* or are the same *in some way. One of* the pictures or drawings does *not* go with the other four — it is *different in some way.*"

● "Which *one* of the five drawings in Question 25 does *not* go with the other four?"

(25)

A	B	C	D	E

Before Question 26, up to and including Question 41, say:

● "And how about in this question?"

(26)

A	B	C	D	E

(27)

A	B	C	D	E

(28)

A	B	C	D	E
V	E	O	N	N

(29)

A	B	C	D	E

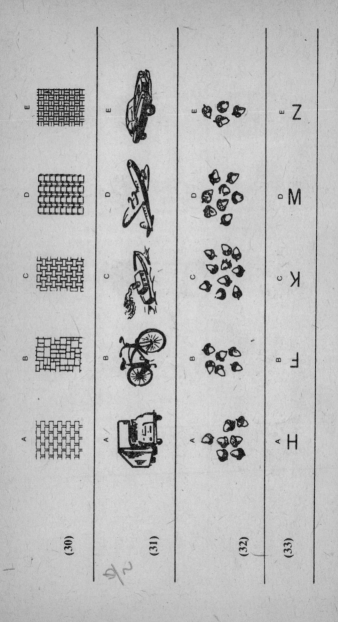

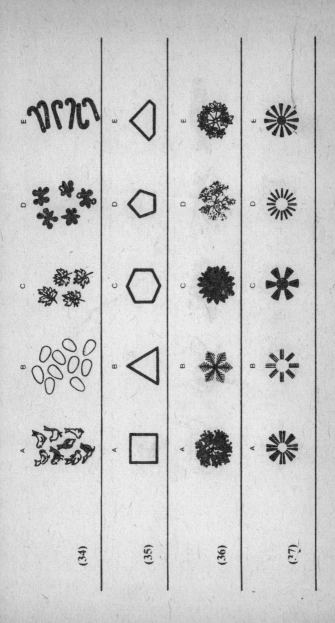

(34)

(35)

(36)

(37)

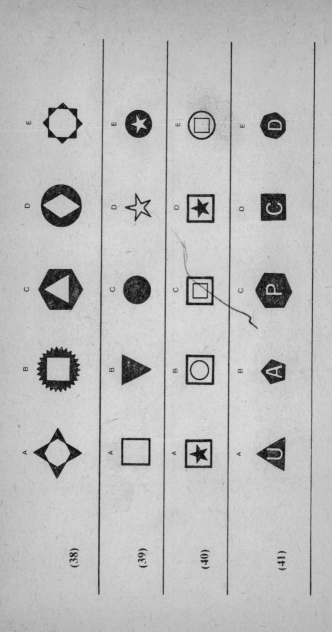

Before Question 42, say:

● "This question is like two that you did before. However, it is harder to answer. How many blocks are there in this picture? Remember that *each block in each layer* above the bottom one has to be supported by one or more blocks under it."

A	B	C	D	E
27	28	29	30	31

(42)

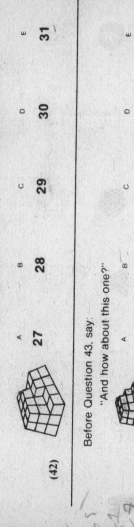

Before Question 43, say:
"And how about this one?"

A	B	C	D	E
68	69	70	71	73

(43)

After finishing Question 43, children below 10½ years of age have completed their portion of the test.

Before Question 44, say:

● "Question 44 is like some questions that you have answered before. Four of the numbers get larger according to some *rule* or *plan* or *pattern*. However, there is one *extra* number that does *not* fit the rule. Which one does *not* fit the rule?"

	A	B	C	D	E
(44)	3	5	7	11	21

Before Question 45, and up to and including Question 55, say:

● "And how about this one?"

	A	B	C	D	E
(45)	29	22	18	15	8
(46)	3	6	10	15	19
(47)	4.6	6.9	9.2	18.4	36.8

	A	B	C	D	E
(48)	8.6	9.9	10.1	11.2	12.5
(49)	2	4	8	12	48
(50)	6,561	3,321	81	9	3
(51)	3	6	8	13	18
(52)	$2\frac{3}{4}$	$1\frac{3}{4}$	$1\frac{1}{2}$	1	$\frac{1}{2}$
(53)	$\frac{1}{2}$	$3\frac{1}{2}$	4	$7\frac{1}{2}$	11

After completing Question 53, children below 14½ years old have finished their portion of the test.

	A	B	C	D	E
(54)	3.00	2.54	1.73	1.32	1.15

	A	B	C	D	E
(55)	$\frac{35}{36}$	$\frac{17}{18}$	$\frac{33}{36}$	$\frac{31}{36}$	$\frac{13}{18}$

END OF TEST

The Key to the Test

The following is a list of the correct answers to the preceding test.

(1) D		(20) B		(39) E	
(2) C		(21) E		(40) C	
(3) D		(22) E		(41) B	
(4) B		(23) D		(42) C	
(5) B		(24) D		(43) B	
(6) D		(25) C		(44) E	
(7) E		(26) C		(45) C	
(8) C		(27) B		(46) E	
(9) A		(28) C		(47) B	
(10) B		(29) A		(48) C	
(11) C		(30) B		(49) C	
(12) C		(31) B		(50) B	
(13) A		(32) A		(51) B	
(14) C		(33) D		(52) C	
(15) D		(34) D		(53) B	
(16) C		(35) E		(54) B	
(17) B		(36) B		(55) C	
(18) E		(37) A			
(19) C		(38) D			

69–71

Marking the Test

In the preceding list of correct answers, the letter given next to each question number indicates the correct response to that specific question. Using a pen or pencil of a different colour ink or lead from the one you used when marking your child's answers, go through the test and circle the question number for each question your child has answered correctly. Remember, the child is allowed only one final answer to each question. In the event two answers have been marked for any single question, that question must be marked as having been answered incorrectly. After you have circled all the questions the child answered correctly, go back and *count the number of questions you have circled as having been answered correctly in the group of questions designated as the questions to be answered for your child's age level*. The total you get is your child's raw score.

Now turn to the interpretation tables on pages 00–00.

Pick out the correct table for your child's age:

TABLE 1

I.Q.s of Children Aged 6 Years 6 Months to 10 Years 6 Months

Questions 1-43	Raw Score												
Child's Age													
6 years 6 months–6 years 9 months	7	10	11	14	15	16	17	18	19	20	21	24	26
6 years 9 months–7 years	9	11	12	15	16	17	18	19	19	20	21	25	26
7 years–7 years 3 months	10	11	12	16	17	18	19	20	21	22	24	26	27
7 years 3 months–7 years 6 months	11	12	14	17	18	19	20	21	22	23	26	26	28
7 years 6 months–7 years 9 months	12	14	16	19	20	21	22	22	23	25	27	28	29
7 years 9 months–8 years	13	15	17	19	20	21	22	23	24	25	27	29	30
8 years–8 years 3 months	14	16	18	20	21	22	23	23	24	25	28	30	31
8 years 3 months–8 years 6 months	14	17	19	20	21	22	23	24	25	26	28	30	32
8 years 6 months–8 years 9 months	15	18	19	20	21	22	23	24	25	26	28	31	32
8 years 9 months–9 years	16	18	20	21	22	23	24	24	25	27	29	31	33
9 years–9 years 3 months	17	18	20	21	22	23	24	25	26	27	29	33	34
9 years 3 months–9 years 6 months	18	19	20	21	22	23	25	25	26	28	29	33	34
9 years 6 months–9 years 9 months	18	19	21	22	23	24	26	26	27	30	31	33	35
9 years 9 months–10 years	19	20	22	23	24	25	27	27	29	31	32	34	36
10 years–10 years 3 months	19	20	22	23	24	25	29	28	29	32	34	35	36
10 years 3 months–10 years 6 months	19	21	23	25	26	27	29	31	30	33	35	36	37
Percentile	2	5	10	20	30	40	50	60	70	80	90	95	98
Approximate I.Q. equivalent	65	73	79	86	91	96	100 - 104		109	114	121	127	133

TABLE 2

I.Q.s of Children Aged 10 Years 6 Months to 14 Years 6 Months

Questions 11–53	Raw Score												
Child's Age													
10 years 6 months–10 years 9 months	8	11	13	17	18	19	20	22	22	23	24	25	27
10 years 9 months–11 years	9	12	15	17	18	19	21	22	23	25	26	27	28
11 years–11 years 3 months	10	12	15	17	18	20	21	22	23	25	28	30	31
11 years 3 months–11 years 6 months	10	13	16	17	19	21	22	23	24	27	28	30	31
11 years 6 months–11 years 9 months	12	13	16	18	20	21	22	23	25	27	29	31	32
11 years 9 months–12 years	12	13	17	20	20	21	22	23	25	27	29	31	32
12 years–12 years 3 months	13	14	17	20	20	21	22	24	25	27	29	31	33
12 years 3 months–12 years 6 months	13	15	17	20	20	21	23	24	26	28	29	31	33
12 years 6 months–12 years 9 months	14	15	18	20	21	22	23	24	26	28	29	31	33
12 years 9 months–13 years	14	15	18	19	21	22	23	25	27	28	30	31	34
13 years–13 years 3 months	14	16	18	20	21	22	24	25	27	28	30	31	34
13 years 3 months–13 years 6 months	15	16	19	20	22	23	24	26	27	29	30	31	34
13 years 6 months–13 years 9 months	15	17	19	21	22	23	25	26	27	29	31	32	35
13 years 9 months–14 years	16	18	20	21	22	24	25	26	27	29	32	32	35
14 years–14 years 3 months	17	19	20	21	23	24	25	26	27	29	32	33	35
14 years 3 months–14 years 6 months	18	19	20	22	23	24	26	27	28	29	32	34	36
Percentile	2	5	10	20	30	40	50	60	70	80	90	95	98
Approximate I.Q. equivalent	65	73	79	86	91	96	100	104	109	114	121	127	133

TABLE 3

I.Q.s OF CHILDREN AGED 14 YEARS 6 MONTHS TO 16 YEARS OR OLDER

Questions 16–55	Raw Score												
Child's Age													
14 years 6 months–15 years	11	12	13	14	17	19	20	21	23	24	26	27	29
15 years–15 years 6 months	12	13	14	15	18	20	21	21	24	25	27	28	29
15 years 6 months–16 years	12	13	14	16	19	20	22	22	25	26	28	28	29
16 years or older	13	14	14	17	19	21	22	23	25	26	28	29	30
Percentile	2	5	10	20	30	40	50	60	70	80	90	95	98
Approximate I.Q. equivalent	65	73	79	86	91	96	100	104	109	114	121	127	133

PART TWO

The Part You *Should* Read:
The Other Side of the Question

CHAPTER FIVE

Are I.Q. Tests Immoral?
Have They Been Debunked?

If I.Q. tests have been successfully debunked and are acknowledged to be of no value, then it logically follows that they cannot be really immoral since they would be ignored.

Over the past several years, we have paid very special attention to the subject of I.Q. and I.Q. testing as it has been reported in all the communications media. Mental testing is 'debunked' with monotonous regularity several times each year. However, the basis for this persistent attack does not seem to arise from new research in the subject area. Writers are usually content to express and re-emphasize doubts that were raised by the pioneers of psychometric testing themselves. Much is made of the argument concerning cultural bias, the critics claiming that this argument not only reduces the validity of the tests but also makes them 'completely meaningless.' The critics are rarely psychologists; often the attacks come from sociologists or political scientists.

This is understandable. Sociological methodology is based on the concept of the individual human being as the unit, the 'atom,' as it were, of a predictable system. Sociological truths are laws concerning the relationships of people and groups, as the laws of chemistry concern the relation of atoms and molecules. Every science must simplify, even over-simplify, before it can begin to deal with the complexity of the world, and the sociological oversimplification is of the equality of all people. Psychometry and psychology, on the other hand, emphasize individual differences – an approach that is inconvenient to sociological theory.

Since sociological theory tends to explain the behaviour of groups in relation to their socioeconomic class and environmental circumstances, it also tends to explain the measurable differences in mental ability as being due to environmental differences often based on socioeconomic status.

Psychometric evidence concedes that this is at least partly true, so some sociologists find it easy to believe that environmental causes are the principal sources of manifest mental differences. They also argue, with some truth, that environmental differences are the ones we can easily do something about and so are most worthy of attention.

There are people of strong political persuasions who claim that since groups from the more privileged socioeconomic classes have a higher average score on tests in general, these tests are used to justify and therefore to perpetuate and exaggerate class privileges. They go on to claim that the identification (or classification) of ability is therefore wrong and should not be allowed at all.

The facts are very different. In reality, people who score well on intelligence tests come from all social and economic backgrounds, and the majority of the gifted individuals in any generation come from less privileged economic groups in that generation. The more privileged groups, however, do contribute a higher *proportion* to the gifted ranks.

Nonetheless, many outspoken professionals believe that any test or procedure that reveals or predicts the underlying differences in human ability is divisive, causing friction between man and his fellow man. However, there is no recent substantive evidence that this is so or that intelligence testing has been used to justify and perpetuate class and racial differences.*

The fiercest divisions do not appear to be those between ability groups but those between formally organized power and pressure groups. There seems to be no special quarrel between the scholars and the dunces in any school, nor any public friction between the middle and working classes. Rather, our age is dominated by a struggle between organized groups, each of which is led by a cadre of tough, intelligent, and able leaders all of whom would undoubtedly do very well on intelligence tests themselves. When the mentally able students get into a conflict, it is not with the less able but with their peers or with even more able professors and lecturers, the so-called 'academic establishments,' which many of them are destined to replace.

An important underlying principle of Western society is the idea of the best man for the job. Only a few rash extremists believe that jobs should be allocated at random, without respect to ability, experi-

*In his much criticized *The Science and Politics of I.Q.*, Professor Kamin quoted a few examples of such arguments up to about 1925, but there are no recent ones. Jensen and Eysenck have suggested that all ethnic groups may not be identical in average I.Q., but we can find no examples of these views being used to justify more privileges for groups with higher average scores.

ence, or competence. Defenders of I.Q. tests claim that they are the fairest methods of assessing one of these qualities, that they are the fairest to all social classes, and that they reflect, less than any other method, the social background of the candidate.

A criticism of I.Q. tests that *is* justified is the argument 'Intelligence is not everything.' The debunkers point out, quite truthfully, that intelligence is not the only quality required by leaders, experts, administrators, technicians, or specialists. They are not so unwise as to say that intelligence is not required for these jobs, but they simply emphasize that other qualities such as humanity, patience, diligence, honesty, and ambition are also important. This appears to be an area of common ground. Few defenders of I.Q. tests will claim that intelligence is the only quality required, although some, with justification, contend that the probability is slightly higher that the other qualities required will be available in highly intelligent people.

Opponents of I.Q. testing also emphasize creativity as a very important quality that is not discovered by I.Q. tests. Creativity is a quality ascribed to artistic and inventive people, those who have a very fluent and imaginative stream of ideas. Critics of I.Q. testing set up creative ability against intelligence, as though there were some kind of competition between the two that creativity is going to win.

J. W. Getzels and B. W. Jackson showed, in their book entitled *Creativity and Intelligence* (John Wiley & Sons, New York, 1962), that those who are in the top 20 per cent for creativity, as they measured it, and who are also below the top 20 per cent for intelligence, did as well as those with the reverse configuration in a variety of tests.

Other researchers have shown that intelligence and creativity are not mutually exclusive but show a marked overlap. Getzels and Jackson not only left out the large majority who did badly on both tests, but they also omitted the small but important group that was in the top 20 per cent on both tests. It would be very interesting to learn how *they* did.

Many experts, on the other hand, feel that creativity as a measurable quality is somewhat doubtful. S. P. Marland, Jr., United States commissioner of education, in his report to Congress entitled *Education of the Gifted and Talented* (March 1972), points out that there is more agreement or correlation between various tests of intelligence and various tests of creativity than there is among the creativity tests themselves when correlated with each other.

Those who believe in and emphasize the importance of creativity over the importance of intelligence make much of the difference between what is called *convergent* and *divergent* intelligence. They point out that I.Q. tests frequently involve choosing the correct answer, or the best answer, from a number of possible alternatives that are given. In other words, the person being tested *converges* on the best answer from a number of possible answers. This very normal activity in problem solving has been labelled *convergent thinking* as opposed to *divergent thinking*, which is rather loosely defined as the activity of producing many ideas from one starting point.

In fact, these two types of thinking are not in opposition, since the process of solving a problem nearly always involves both kinds of activity. Once the problem has been presented and understood, the second stage, in the solver's mind, is that of casting round in the memory of imagination among a number of potential solutions to the problem. Obviously, the more prolific a person is in producing the tryout ideas, the better chance he has of finding the correct or best solution. This stage, which is often quite unconscious, can be said to be the *divergent stage* in the problem solving process. Starting with the original problem solving area, the solver spreads out an array of potential solutions. The next stage of the problem solving process is the elimination of all but one of the options created at the first stage by using intelligent judgment. This is the *convergent* stage. When the optimum option has been chosen, problem solving stops and action begins.

In the convergent type of intelligence test, the problem setter himself may take over his job and give a number of alternatives in the setting out of the problem itself.

In the debate that is developing between the supporters of convergent and the supporters of divergent thinking, these two necessary parts of problem solving are thought of as two different kinds of mental ability. It is suggested that the searching, experimental activity that generates possible solutions is to be valued more than the discriminatory activity of choosing the correct or best answer.

It has also been suggested that yet another type of thinking process has not been taken into account in I.Q. tests. It is labelled *lateral* thinking and refers to the type of mental jump from problem to solution or to a new approach that sometimes happens when the approach is not obvious.

When a solver is working on a problem where no remembered or logical approach seems promising, it has been suggested that the solver should strike off at random and think about apparently unassociated ideas. This is obviously good advice so long as people do not start searching in the less hopeful low-chance regions without first systematically having explored the more obvious approaches. Lateral thinking is clearly a last resort.

There is also a school of thought that relies on challenging the definition of intelligence or, more frequently, on saying that the concept of intelligence is undefinable and therefore meaningless. They point to the fact that the word in its modern sense of mental ability has had a number of definitions that do not agree with each other. This fact is used to throw doubt on the validity of the concept itself. Some of these people even dismiss human intelligence as an elitist trick to persuade people to accept economic inequality. Their argument goes: There is no agreed-on definition of intelligence; therefore, there is no such thing as intelligence. But there are many things that obviously exist but are very hard to define. H. G. Wells once pointed out that there is no definition of a chair, or *chairishness*, that he could not, with the help of a good carpenter, defeat. But that fact should not suspend our belief in chairs.

Do you feel that the people you have met in life are all alike in their ability to solve problems, to understand relationships, to learn facts, and generally use their minds? If you do, then you must agree with the debunkers. But if you ever catch yourself saying things such as 'Jack is rather bright and Jill is a bit of a fool' or 'Tom is an idiot and Fred is a clever so-and-so,' then at least your mind must be open to the suggestion that these judgments are based on some kind of unconscious assessment that people vary in some way. It follows that, underneath at least, you believe that intelligence and ability are not dished out by God on a strict fair shares rationing basis.

Equality

Those people who declare that I.Q. tests are immoral say that by setting up a measurement relating to mental ability, the tester has committed an act of discrimination and has emphasized individual differences by assigning a rank and number to them.

Have you ever heard of an underground war between athletes and cripples, fast and slow runners, the short and the tall, the skinny and the fat, or, indeed, between the blonds and the brunettes in any street, club, or school? It simply does not seem to be true that revealing such differences between people necessarily creates strife.

Even if we refuse to measure differences in mental ability, they will still be spotted and recognized, because nothing will stop people from observing and judging one another. What will be lost, however, is any accuracy and impartiality in these assessments. We shall also fail to recognize potential that is not always shown in early performance.

Perhaps we should look at the idea of equality again. The word is not always used in the same way. Political equality can be used to describe affairs where the political influence, rights, and opportunities available to every citizen are equal. Equality can also be extended to suggest that people's income and privileges should be equal. It can be yet further extended to suggest (and this is the extremist position) that all people are in fact equal in every way, or that any differences between them are unimportant and can be ignored.

Politicians and moralists who favour these various increasing extensions of equality always argue that acceptance of their ideas will reduce conflict. Their arguments, however, seem to be based on assumptions, not actual experience.

Social animals that live in herds, tribes, or cooperating groups have the problem of avoiding all-out competition and mutual destruction among the various members. Prominent, of course, among these social animals is man himself.

What is observed in every type of social, living animal, from invertebrates up to man, is that a simple social mechanism is set up – a ranking system or pecking order – by which every animal has an accepted position in the hierarchy of the social group.

Professor Wynne-Edwards observed a fact concerning the life of animals in the wild that was so obvious that it had been invisible to previous observers. He perceived that animals living in the wild without human interference were usually healthy, sleek, and well fed despite the fact that their food supply was limited. According to Thomas Robert Malthus, the nineteenth century British economist, a population will expand until the food supply is inadequate. Therefore, we should expect the natural state of a wild population of animals to be semistarvation. But apparently there are built-in behaviour patterns, like territoriality, pecking order, and mock fighting, which act as a kind of self-regulating system. Instead of semistarvation for the entire species, a pattern arises that means an adequate amount is provided for a limited number and the remainder are naturally eliminated. It works like this: after a series of trial, and relatively harmless, scuffles that consist of display and mock attacks, the animals sort themselves out into a rank order that is well understood and accepted by all of them. The higher ranks have first access to the food and the females of the species, a fact of life conceded by all the lower ranks. The effect of the system is to enable animals to live together in cooperating groups without excessive and damaging fighting, which would undermine the survival of the whole group.

If a social group comes upon hard times, such as food shortages, there are alternatives. The members of the group can fight among themselves until they are debilitated and make easy prey for their enemies. Alternatively, they can have an equal sharing system, which might mean having a subsistence ration for half the winter and none for the rest. The last alternative is a behaviour pattern that insures that some still will be fully fed and retain their capacity for flight and fight. The unfortunate lower status animals perish, but the tribe or herd survives as a whole.

The lesson to be learned from this is simple: because of seasonal ups and downs and the accidents of life, it seems that, in their natural surroundings, animals that live in herds and groups find that it is *equality* that is divisive and *inequality* that makes social life possible.

A society dedicated to the principle of total equality among its members is fighting to maintain an unstable situation. It will pay the price with a certain, though perhaps acceptable, increase in internal conflict. There is certainly no sign of reduced conflict in the increasingly egalitarian and affluent societies of the West. Most disputes between men and management are about *differentials* – that is, about adjustments in the pecking order. The moral and emotional force behind status-preserving conflict is the strongest we encounter.

The moral values of our society – liberty, equality, and fraternity – are good and desirable, but we maintain them only by constant struggle against the biological pressure to return to a stable state of inequality. This morally desirable, unstable state, however, will only be maintained by ethical and moral traditions less available to other animals.

We men and women take it for granted that the adults, the strong and able in each generation, must support, lead, maintain, and nurture the young, whose abilities have not fully developed, and the old, whose abilities are in decay. We often do not see clearly that the ablest among the adults must make more than their fair contribution for the good of all. And we also sometimes fail to see that those who can do so much for all are worth the special attention of our educators.

It is, perhaps, the tacit realization of the inherent instability of equality as a social principle that gives force to some of the unreasoning attacks upon intelligence testing.

In his book *I.Q. in the Meritocracy*, R. J. Herrnstein recounts how he published an article about the history of intelligence testing and summarized the main facts that have accumulated in the technical literature for several generations about the inheritance of I.Q. and the social class differences involved. After the publication of his article, Herrnstein was subjected to a widespread campaign of academic vilification. His opponents seemed not to have troubled to read what he had actually written. Without exception all the remarks published that were attributed to him were misquotations. He was accused of racism, though he had not touched upon the subject of race at all. The campaign was led by a small group of activists, and a number of Herrnstein's lectures, which were in no way connected with I.Q. testing, were packed with protesters and had to be abandoned. A more recent example has been the attempted character assassination of Sir Cyril Burt.

As shocking as this extreme behaviour may seem, it happened, and it serves as an example of the conflict that has boiled around the use of I.Q. tests and the release of their results.

As you can now readily see, the arguments against intelligence tests are not consistent, nor do the critics present a cohesive, logical, or objective argument. Rather, they constitute a number of disjointed, sporadic, and often mutually contradictory attacks. The theory on which intelligence testing is based takes into consideration these divergent points of view, assimilates their intrinsic value or importance, and logically evaluates before analysing results.

To summarize the arguments that are brought forward and that do not add up:

1. Intelligence tests are supposed to measure intelligence, and *intelligence* is undefined.
2. The definition of the quality *intelligence* is contradictory.
3. Intelligence tests only measure the subject's ability to do intelligence tests.
4. Intelligence tests measure nothing at all. (The quality they are supposed to measure, intelligence, does not exist.)
5. The quality intelligence tests are supposed to measure, intelligence, is not important.
6. Creativity is more important than intelligence.
7. Lateral thinking is more important than intelligence.
8. Other things are important as well as intelligence.
9. Intelligence tests are used to perpetuate racist and class privilege.
10. The statistical background of intelligence tests is faulty and they are discredited.
11. Intelligence tests are unreliable.
12. Intelligence tests are unfair to underprivileged groups.
13. Intelligence tests have no predictive value at all.
14. Intelligence tests are self-fulfilling predictions.
15. Intelligence tests measure only the effect of social background.
16. Intelligence tests are of no value and can be disregarded.
17. Intelligence tests are used to label children.
18. Intelligence tests are used to prepare children for an unjust society.

When we see these arguments lined up, we begin to see a degree of overkill that makes us suspicious of the whole thing. For smallpox there is one simple preventive remedy, vaccination. For the common cold, which we cannot cure, there are a thousand remedies. Intelligence testing survives the ceaseless assaults of its critics, and we might suspect that the long continual virulence and persistence of the attack is a partial proof of that very attack's failure.

Opponents of I.Q. testing object that the tests 'label' children. The idea is that by revealing the potential ability in some children, you unavoidably show up the lower potential ability in others. They are labelled as potential failures, and this becomes a self-fulfilling prophecy. The child's teacher lowers his expectations for the less able child, and this in itself results in different academic achievements and even in different subsequent I.Q. scores.

There is a very much publicized finding by Rosenthal and Jacobsen, who claim that experiments reveal what they call a 'Pygmalion effect.' Teachers were given deceptive information leading them to have a false expectation that certain children were 'spurters' with high I.Q.s and that they would do well later. The children were tested several times over a two-year teaching period. It was claimed that the result of this experiment was that the children tended to fulfil the expectations based on the misinformation and that those labelled 'spurters' did improve in their I.Q. scores. From this it was deduced that teachers' expectations have a considerable effect on I.Q. scores, and as a result children get into self-confining ruts based on a teacher's classification.

The soundness of this experiment has been severely questioned by many experts, but it would seem that doing away with I.Q. testing can only make matters worse. If the children's performance is based on the teacher's expectations and we refuse to give the teacher any objective information, then he or she will be forced to rely only upon his or her own subjective judgment; this has been shown often to be even less reliable than the relatively objective I.Q. test. The experiments do, however, present a very good argument against giving teachers misinformation about children.

Nonetheless, whether we accept the Pygmalion effect or not, the results of this experiment clearly demonstrate the need for *correct* assessment and frequent rechecking. They certainly do not bring down the large edifice of work on the assessment of intelligence and ability built up over three-quarters of a century by many psychologists.

Perhaps we should look more closely at the idea of labelling – what it implies and why it is objected to.

In any education system, there are more pupils than teachers. Each teacher has to deal with between a dozen and fifty children and must use appropriate methods. It is impossible for the teacher to establish the same kind of relationship with every child that the parent has. The teacher can try to treat each child exactly alike and work on the assumption of uniformity, or he can try as best he can to take account of the individual differences between the children as far as he can perceive and understand them. If any testing or assessment instruments, such as I.Q. and personality tests, are available, he can make use of this information.

In practice, every teacher has to assume a position between these two extremes. In different eras, educators have tended to go one way or the other. The 'treat them all alike' school has favoured strict discipline, stern punishment, and the concept of the child as an empty vessel that has to be filled with knowledge by the all-knowing teacher. The modern educators in the Western world tend toward the other extreme and place a great emphasis on the individual differences of children and the need to understand these children as unique persons who require individual assessment and treatment.

The paradox of modern education is that the teacher is trying to work with two contradictory notions – the notion of equality, which says that all children are of equal potential and value, and the philosophy that each child is unique and entirely different from every other child and requires a completely individual approach. They have determined to try to understand each child as an individual, but their love of equality forces them to try to believe that all children are indistinguishable in that particular human quality that is most important in education – intelligence, or educability. The teachers have available to them evidence that is at least objective, though admittedly not infallible, concerning this most important individual difference between children. Hopefully, teachers will use this information in ways that will prove most beneficial to your children, for if it is used in a positive framework, knowledge of intelligence abilities can serve as an effective means of encouragement for the bright child and the underachiever as well.

CHAPTER SIX

What to Do About
the Gifted Child

The shape of the bell curve makes it reasonable to
predict that most parents who read this book and
test their children will find that their children are
reassuringly average. But *some* parents will discover that these tests reveal a very high I.Q. or
percentile rating. The probability is that these
parents have a gifted child in their family – a
problem, a joy, and a great responsibility. Any
percentile rating over the 95th should alert parents to this possibility.

In the report *Education of the Gifted and Talented* submitted by the United States commissioner of education, S. P. Marland, Jr., to the U.S.
Congress in March 1972, Marland says:

> We know that gifted children can be identified
> as early as the pre-school grades and that these
> children in later life often make outstanding
> contributions to our society in the arts, politics,
> business and the sciences. But, disturbingly,
> research has confirmed that many talented
> children perform far below their intellectual
> potential. We are increasingly being stripped of
> the comfortable notion that a bright mind will
> make its own way. Intellectual and creative

talent cannot survive educational neglect and apathy.

The Marland report goes on to say, 'This loss is particularly evident in the minority groups who have, in both social and educational environments, every configuration calculated to stifle potential talent.' Under the heading 'Summary and Major Findings,' the report continues:

There can be few, if any, exceptions to the observations threading through this study, that the gifted and talented youth are a unique population, differing markedly from their age peers in abilities, talent, interests, and psychological maturity. The most versatile and complex of all human groups, they suffer the neglect that is typical of all groups with special educational needs. Their sensitivity to others and insight into existing school conditions, make them especially vulnerable; they frequently conceal their giftedness in standardized surroundings. The resultant waste in human terms and national resources is tragic.

The relatively few gifted students who have had the advantage of special programmes, have shown remarkable improvements in self-understanding and in ability to relate to others, as well as in improved academic and creative performance.

But many young people go unnoticed. In the United Kingdom, the Department of Education and Science Pamphlet, Summer 1975, points out in the introduction that the education of gifted children is becoming a greater focus of concern among teachers and parents. There is an increasing awareness that these children have special educational needs, and disquiet as to whether the present provisions meet them appropriately.

At school the proportion of gifted pupils who remain unrecognized is unknown, but the evidence indicates that it is probably considerable, particularly among children coming from poor families, and immigrants; environmental deprivation has its most adverse effect on the scholastic performance of the brightest children, not the average or dull. Better techniques of identification and their use by teachers (who should be on the alert for these children) are necessary.

Most European countries have elite secondary schools where the more able children, about 20 per cent, can obtain entrance at the ages between ten and twelve. The highly gifted child is very likely to go to these schools and is gradually selected by clearing successive hurdles as he goes through the system of school and university. However, most countries in northern Europe are in the process of transforming their system of secondary education into a comprehensive one (i.e., one type of school for all children regardless of ability), thus, they are coming up against the problem of the gifted child in such a system.

In Sweden, where this process has advanced the furthest, they do not differentiate the gifted at any early age but split the children into broad bands of ability during the seventh, eighth, and ninth years, directing the appropriate streams toward university education.

In France, children are differentiated by type of course, and the lycées are selected by the middle class parents whom they serve. But the French are moving toward a more comprehensive system, like the U.K. and Scandinavia. (They have, however, a severe problem in trying to work an undiscriminating university system.)

In Italy an attempt to run universities without selection is said to have led to a serious deterioration in standards so that many qualifications are little valued.

In Russia, all children go to a neighbourhood eight year school, but there are special arrangements for the very gifted. There are four special schools that are really university boarding schools. They are in Novosibirsk, Kiev, Moscow, and Leningrad. These schools cater to gifted children from rural areas only. Recruitment in Russia is by competitive examination where mathematics and physics are the deciding subjects.

Although each country has its own approach to the problem, they all share the common dilemma of a very special problem that has been created by the drive toward educational egalitarianism.

It is, undoubtedly, the increasing problem concerning gifted children that has motivated the setting up of the gifted children's movements in many countries.

The first gifted children's movements began in the United States and were well established by the early sixties. In Britain the National Association for Gifted Children was set up in March 1966. A World Council for the Gifted was established after the World Congress on Gifted Children held in London in September 1975. It seems likely that this movement, for which the initiative came from the British National Association for Gifted Children under the directorship of Henry Collis, will be a very influential one.

Parents may ask why this movement has acquired its particular name. The term *gifted* as a description for very bright children has been adopted rather than *intelligent* or *able* because the term is intended to have a broader range and thus include children with talents other than those clearly associated with intelligence (which is seen as problem solving ability and the ability to see and understand relationships). However, the meaning attached to the word *gifted* does not really include *all* the gifted or exceptionally able. Usually, for instance, athletic skills are not included in the meaning. The principal types of giftedness that *are* included, other than those specifically associated with intelligence itself, are artistic and musical talents. All authorities seem to be dissatisfied with the vagueness of the definition of giftedness, and there is considerable disagreement.

More precision could be brought to the definition of giftedness if it were more clearly seen that there are essentially three ways in which children can excel – ways in which their performance can be termed excellent, or exceptionally able.

The three apparently independent directions of ability are:

1. Those associated with skilful, coordinated

use of the body, as in sports and mechanical skills.

2. Those associated with an urge to create – innovate, draw, paint, make music.

3. Those associated with intellectual functions – the ability to think, to reason, to see relationships, to draw conclusions, to classify information correctly and to solve problems.

This last direction – intellectual ability – might almost be called data processing ability.

Considerable experimentation has shown that there is some correlation between these various abilities, but this correlation is difficult to establish because for psychomotor ability and artistic ability there exist a few properly standardized methods of measurement. In addition, most authorities agree that the development of psychomotor skills, which occurs very early in life, is a separate process not closely bound up with the development of intelligence itself. On psychomotor tests, baby monkeys can beat human babies quite easily.

The Marland report states that performance tests designed to measure general intelligence have been the most widely used criteria of giftedness both in research and selection. This has occurred because these tests are so widely available.

With regard to the level of selection, there is a tendency to accept the criterion established by Terman in his original study on gifted California children. This method determines giftedness at the I.Q. level 140. In other words, about four children per thousand are in this group and are considered to be the most highly gifted school children. However, other authorities place the lower limit of giftedness at the 98th percentile (the Mensa level; see page 21).

It is preferable to choose the lower level simply because the normal standard intelligence test is quite good at identifying the top 5 per cent or the top 2 per cent of high ability children, but it becomes far less certain when we attempt to discriminate above that level. It would be better to use a number of different tests. For very high levels of intelligence, tests such as those developed by Professor Alice Heim in England are preferable because they are designed to discriminate at a high level. Unfortunately, these are only applicable to older children.

Perhaps one of the best definitions of giftedness is the legal definition employed in Illinois.

Gifted children are those children whose mental development is accelerated beyond the average to the extent that they need and can profit from specially planned educational services.

The problem of identifying the gifted is not easy. The Marland report points out that some young people with potential mask their abilities in order to adapt to the group they are working in. Others cannot find an outlet in school for their particular talents.

To help you in your determination of your child's abilities, there is the following check list of twenty points to watch for in your children. If your children are gifted, they may:

1. Possess superior powers of reasoning, of dealing with abstractions, of generalizing from specific facts, of understanding meanings, and of seeing into relationships
2. Have great intellectual curiosity
3. Learn easily and readily
4. Have a wide range of interests
5. Have a broad attention span that enables them to concentrate and persevere in solving problems and pursuing interests
6. Be superior in the quantity and quality of vocabulary as compared with other children of their own age
7. Have ability to do effective work independently
8. Have learned to read early (often well before school age)
9. Exhibit keen powers of observation
10. Show initiative and originality in intellectual work
11. Show alertness and quick response to new ideas
12. Be able to memorize quickly
13. Have great interest in the nature of man and the universe (problems of origins and destiny, and so on)
14. Possess unusual imagination
15. Follow complex directions easily
16. Be rapid readers
17. Have several hobbies
18. Have reading interests that cover a wide range of subjects
19. Make frequent and effective use of the library

20. Be superior in mathematics, particularly in problem solving

Can teachers spot gifted children? Marland quotes from several surveys where teachers did not, on the average, appear to be very good at identifying children with the ability to score well. Only one-fifth of the superior boys and two-fifths of the superior girls were described as precocious or mentally quick. Yet these children were at the one-in-a-thousand level on the mental ability test. Some of those very bright children were even classed as dull or mentally sluggish.

Ignoring teachers' impressions, scientific personality tests were applied to all the children, and the conclusions were very obvious indeed. The exceptionally bright children stood out from the children with lower scores, on the average, in every respect and were rated to have a significantly 'superior' personality from the point of view of the experimenters. The characteristic that stood out most was adventurousness. A substantially higher proportion of the very gifted group were said to be adventurous – more than twice as many as those who scored in the top 10 per cent. The bright children were classed as being ambitious, dependable, energetic, friendly, happy, honest, and investigative. They were leaders; they liked jokes; they were original; they were polite and tidy. Obviously, these characteristics did not apply to all the high scoring children. These were the comments that were most frequently made about that group in comparison with the lower scoring children.

The evidence from a number of studies is perhaps the strongest ground for the view that the group of children that is potentially of most value to the next generation is the very highly gifted.

One speaker at the World Congress for Gifted Children spoke of children being 'severely gifted' and felt that they ought to be looked at as an especially disadvantaged group for whom special treatment would be both wise and appropriate. Just as we treat the mentally or physically handicapped with special educational facilities, so too should we provide the gifted with special educational opportunities. It is clearly to our advantage to exploit this the most precious of the resources available to us.

It is our duty to foster the development of exceptional talents for the benefit of the next generation. Parents who are fortunate enough to have a child in the highly gifted range on these tests should gain the attention of those responsible for the child's education and get in touch with their local gifted children's association.

One of the tragic facts to emerge from Project Talent, a survey conducted on four hundred and fifty thousand secondary students throughout the United States, was that parents are not at all good at spotting talents in their own children. Only 17 per cent of the parents of highly gifted children desired a higher level of education for the children. Even worse, 18 per cent of the parents, as a whole, set their ambitions for the education of their children at very low levels or had no ambition for them at all.

The failure of parents to stimulate gifted children leads to an enormous waste of talent. The critical importance of early stimulation for children was pointed out by Sir John Eccles in *Facing Reality*. He showed that the actual development of the nervous system is physically inhibited by lack of stimulation. He experimented with a group of mice, covering one eye and leaving one eye with normal sight on each mouse. The number of synaptic knobs on the nerve dendrites in the normal visual cortex of mice twenty-four and forty-eight days old respectively was extremely depleted in each case in areas associated with the blind eyes. Those associated with the effective eye were very much richer in dentritic spines, which, in turn, are associated with mental action. A similar phenomenon has been noticed with animals brought up in the dark. The evidence indicates that those dendrite buds that do not develop properly because of lack of stimulation cannot later be developed if stimulation happens after the latency period in very early life.

S. P. Marland, Jr., stated that the majority of the gifted were underachievers in that their attainments, although much higher than those of the rest of the school population, were very much below their potential. These underachievers suffered greatly from a lack of stimulation. Those that did appear to be achieving their potential were examined for any factors that might be relevant. The factor that emerged most strongly was that 74 per cent of the high achieving group of gifted children had some person, described as a mentor, who took a special interest in the child. These mentors were often parents but sometimes teachers, sometimes favourite uncles, and sometimes casual friends. The mentors appeared to be people of intelligence and discernment who had spotted talent in the child and were doing their best to foster it.

Obviously, the best possible person to be a mentor to a child is the parent. The idea of calling on someone from outside might be distasteful to many, but sensible parents who recognize their own limitations will want to use such outside help. No parent should object to consulting a doctor or psychiatrist when he recognizes that his own medical and psychological skills are not enough. Parents who feel that they do not have the time, knowledge, ability, or interest to develop the educational and intellectual interest of their children can find others who have all these qualities and who are very willing to help. I must emphasize, however, that selecting a mentor is a delicate process. The bringing together of gifted children and suitable mentors is a matter requiring the skill of a qualified professional.

If a child is highly gifted, its career prospects are greater than average. In California between 1925 and 1968, Terman and Oden selected a group of ten-year-old children and another group of fifteen-year-olds on the basis of a score at the level of 140 I.Q. There were fourteen hundred and seventy subjects selected from a population of one million.

Twenty-five years later, 71 per cent of this group were in professional, semi-professional, or managerial occupations, compared with 13·7 per cent of the California population as a whole. Their average income was higher than the typical college graduate's.

In another aspect of this study, the most successful and the least successful 20 per cent of the gifted group were compared. Ratings by parents, spouses, and the subjects themselves showed that what was lacking in the unsuccessful group was perseverance and integration toward goals. In addition, they tended to suffer from inferiority feelings.

The evidence accumulated by Terman and Oden can be summed up as follows: most of the gifted do become successful according to the usual criteria, but the 20 per cent of the gifted who do not succeed do not feel themselves to be failures. They have often deliberately shunned the pursuit of occupational success. The successful group tended to come from stable, middle class homes where books were available and where parents emphasized the importance of education and had high expectations for their children. In such homes, children developed strong intellectual interests and strong drives for achievement. (Sad to say, about half of the gifted women in the sample had remained in the home.)

These general conclusions were noted by the British Department of Education:

1. There is a strong tendency for children to fulfil early promise; their performance in later years reflects early performance indications.
2. The best indication of how a child will develop at school is given by intelligence tests. They are better than personality tests or other types of assessment.
3. High I.Q. alone does not guarantee success. The child needs ambition to do well – the drive and determination to succeed.

4. Family background and environment are vital. They are the most important factors in how well a bright child realizes his promise.
5. Very bright children may be of equal intellectual ability but they are extraordinarily different in personality, interests, and achievement.

In the modern world, which is so devoted to the idea of equality, there is a very real problem for the parents and educators of gifted children. Ideas of justice and social equality have created a drive toward homogeneous mixed ability classes in comprehensive schools to which all children must go. The educational system in some countries is being pushed into this mould at a rate many people think is dangerously fast. Bright students are now likely to be submerged in these schools, where the opportunities to receive the special teaching and stimulation they require are likely to be significantly reduced.

This tendency places a special extra responsibility on parents. It means they should try to produce the needed extra stimulus and challenge outside the school environment. Responsible associations for gifted children strongly recommend that bright children be brought together into classes outside school hours where they can benefit from mutual stimulus and challenge and where they can be taught by teachers who can become skilled in the special problems of the gifted.

Whatever the moral arguments are against segregating gifted children, there can be little argument about the success of the system introduced many generations ago, which produced highly educated and able scholars and administrators – an intellectual cadre that has been of inestimable value to society. It is important that we do not dry up the supply altogether by ignoring the able and gifted students. We need an improvement, not a reduction, in the quality of education and in the supply of highly educated people to do the complicated work of a complex society. The work of Terman finally dispelled the myth that the highly intelligent are somehow odd, puny, or unhealthy. Neither are they necessarily from the upper class economically. An examination of forty-five thousand children, in over four hundred and fifty-five schools and three hundred and ten communities, carried out by the Co-ordinated Studies in Education Incorporated showed that the popular opinion that the most superior children came from upper class homes was far from the truth. All the very superior children, at levels up to one in a thousand, were rated as to the social and economic background of the parents, the father's occupation, the possession of middle class implements (telephone, car, radio, and amount of living space occupied).

The results were unequivocal. The children who, on objective selection tests, turned out to be the most gifted group of all, came from parents from the full range of social and occupational classes. The possible home background class ratings ranged from 0 to 18, and the gifted group spanned the range from 2 to 15. The same point is raised by Eysenck in his book *The Inequality of Man*, where he states that all social and occupational classes contribute to the pool of the gifted.

Terman's analysis of the life history of the one hundred and fifty most successful and one hundred and fifty least successful among the very gifted adult males he studied since childhood is very interesting. The group with the better social and emotional adjustment was overwhelmingly the most successful group. This raises the question of the effect of putting a brilliant child into a class of normal children. The sharp contrast between the child and its peers may represent a handicap that holds the child back in its development and thus denies to society as a whole the full fruit of its talents.

One should ask whether enough is done for the gifted. Considering that gifted children are those who can contribute most to the prosperity and stability of the world in the next generation; and remembering that it is they who can do most to solve the serious problems that confront humanity, we might reasonably expect that all possible aid be given to these exceptional children to help them fulfil their potential. If one looks at the amount of money spent as an indication of the effort made, then certainly society has no such view. The Marland report notes that in twenty-seven school districts in the U.S. that have programmes for gifted children, the expenditure per pupil on the intellectually gifted was ninety-two dollars. Compare this expenditure with the approximately $721 spent on each mentally retarded pupil and $1729 for each physically handicapped pupil. In the U.K. despite the efforts of the National Association for Gifted Children, very little is being done, and such children often find themselves left to study on their own.

Frequently, teachers have to rely on their unaided judgment, and experience shows that teachers are able to identify only about half the gifted. When it comes to identifying the *highly* gifted, it was shown that 25 per cent of the most gifted were missed altogether.

In a programme conducted by Dr Bridges known as the Brentwood experiment, a group of gifted children were withdrawn from their own schools for one afternoon a week for thirty weeks each year. The level chosen was an I.Q. of 140 and over, and a pilot group and two other groups were experimented with over a number of years.

The problem that immediately emerged was that it was difficult to find teachers for these gifted children. Some teachers were astounded and alarmed by the speed with which some children answered questions. The teachers felt they would not have the quickness of mind to deal with such children.

It became very clear that being educated among normal children, the gifted became accustomed to a lower level of expectation by teachers and parents, so that the gifted students' demands upon themselves were very low. The effect of mixing them in with other gifted children was to raise their own aspirations and make them more self-critical. Another thing revealed by their being taught with normal children was the tendency to impatience. The gifted children quickly mastered what the teacher was trying to put over, got tired, and became bored. Dr Bridges felt that this situation might lead to the development of a 'butterfly mind' – one that has trouble concentrating – unless the child could be given sufficient challenge and stimulation.

In his experiments on the gifted children who had been selected, Dr Bridges found that although most of them were moderately popular in their own schools, some were almost completely isolated from the other children. In this respect, the findings concur with the Marland report because after a period away at the Brentwood classes, these previously isolated gifted children began integrating much better with their peers in their own school, and, contrary to what might be expected, the other children in the school did not show any signs of resentment toward those who had been chosen for the gifted children's experiment. The teachers confirmed this finding.

The saddest thing that Dr Bridges discovered was that gifted children often incurred the resentment and jealousy of their *parents* and of their *teachers*. One family whose child had an I.Q. of 170 was not pleased at having a bright child but upset, bewildered, and annoyed by his quickness of thought, which they could not match. Much worse was the case of one bright child selected for Dr Bridges's experiments who was often scolded by the teacher at his normal school until he dissolved into tears. His behaviour at the classes with other gifted children was exemplary.

The most serious problem was summed up by Dr Bridges:

Our finding has been that underachievement can occur when a bright child has powers much in excess of what he is called on to use in school: such a child may be first in his class and still, from the viewpoint of his intellectual gifts, be underachieving. In such cases the measure of underachievement is obscured by the general satisfaction of a relatively good achievement. Underachievement, therefore, may go unrecognized, so that a child coasts along quite satisfactorily but with little use of his powers.

Dr Bridges referred to what he called the 'stint,' or given level of achievement that gifted children often set up for themselves, which was often far below the level of their potential achievement.

Being accustomed to easy success among normal children, the gifted students at Dr Bridges's school had to learn that mistakes and failures were not all-important. The gifted children had to be *taught* to set their sights higher. However, Bridges pointed out that the level of difficulty must not be raised too high or the child pushed too fast. It was essential that the child had a certain level of success all the time; otherwise, he or she would become discouraged. There was the rarer, but still existent, problem of overchallenging the gifted child so that it got discouraged by too long a succession of failures.

Dr Bridges was very firm on one point. He said that the gifted child needed more teaching, not less teaching, than the normal child and that the idea that the gifted child would make its own way and manage on its own was completely fallacious.

In *How to Raise a Brighter Child*, Joan Beck points out that the best time for many kinds of learning and, more important, for stimulating the basic learning abilities, is already passed by the time the child reaches five years of age and enters school. Unavoidably, every parent has the important responsibility of setting the stage in these early years for the child's performance during the rest of its life.

All studies concur in their findings that these early formative years are of the utmost importance. This means that the child's future ability and effectiveness is very much affected by his preschool home environment. Very bright children can be taught to read and deal with numbers from as early as three to four years old, and there is no evidence supporting those who would claim that this can be harmful. On the contrary, those who are given an early opportunity to learn seem to benefit from this all their lives.

Joan Beck's views, as a result of her experience with bright young children, is that most people greatly underestimate what children under five can and should be learning. She feels that these children's intelligence, enthusiasm, and happiness can be greatly improved by more intensive methods of early education.

Young children, and especially intelligent young children, need stimulation and excitement. The urge to explore, experiment, examine, probe, be into everything, and, yes, take everything to pieces, is as right and natural as hunger and thirst. It is necessary to the development of the child that it be given plentiful opportunities to explore everything around it and to keep its mind occupied with a constant succession of fresh images and opportunities.

In addition, child care theories that discourage parents from 'overstimulating' the child are quite likely to do more harm than good. The old fear of putting pressure on children is gradually fading as the results of this policy become clear. There is a return to the idea that there can be no harm in satisfying a child's curiosity and eagerness for learning.

The lesson for parents is very clear. Your child needs plenty of stimulation and interest to feed its curiosity. If you have reason to believe it is a gifted child, it is even more important for it to gain early experience and knowledge. Your child can begin to learn its letters and numbers as soon as you like. It needs pictures, books, travel, and experience as much as it needs food and medical care.

CHAPTER SEVEN

What to Do About the Retarded

Mental deficiency, mental defect, retardation, mental handicap, feeblemindedness – these are some of the many labels given to a clearly definable condition noticed in a small proportion of children. If the evidence of this test gives you even a slight suspicion that your child falls into this class, seek expert guidance immediately.

The first person to see is your doctor. Some experts believe that the condition results only from some disturbance or abnormality – a defect in the organization of the brain that may either be due to brain damage or be inborn. The other view is that the condition is usually due to the normal variability of human intelligence and simply represents the lower tail of the normal distribution curve. Most experts seem to think that both views are valid and that they are not mutually exclusive. There can be pathological and familial reasons in different cases, or in many cases, there can be a combination of both reasons. There is also an argument on the effect of upbringing on a child and the extent to which mental defects can be attributed to it, and there is evidence that brain damaged children who have been institutionalized do visibly worse than those who have had individual care in good families.

The genetic contribution to retardedness is well established. Despite the high correlation between low intelligence in the parent and retardedness in the children, retardedness is found in varying proportions in children from parents of all levels of intelligence and from all sections of the community.

The classification of the condition must be arbitrary because one class of feeblemindedness merges into the next. The usual classification is on the basis of I.Q.

I.Q.	Description
70–90	Low
50–70	Retardate
20–50	Imbecile
0–20	Moron

At the lower end of this unhappy scale are the untestables, those whose responses are not adequate to an I.Q. test. There is not much hope for children who are unfortunate enough to be born imbeciles or morons, and generally speaking we can say that the closer to normal the I.Q. score, the greater the possibility of remedial action. However, some remarkable results have been achieved recently with very severely retarded children, but the relative expenditure of time, money, and skill is, alas, often not well rewarded.

Despite the intensive criticism of I.Q. tests as a measure of mental excellence, there is little dispute about their value as a diagnostic tool in dealing with problems of mental retardation. No one in the field of psychiatry seems to be able to propose a better way of distinguishing between the various levels of retardation. Obviously, the administration of an intelligence test becomes progressively more difficult as we approach *either* extreme, and it is perhaps more so when we approach the extreme of mental defects. Therefore, we do not recommend amateur attempts to test I.Q. at any level much below I.Q. 80, the borderline of retardation. If, as a result of testing your child, you find the result is anywhere in that region, you must consider the possibility of faults in your procedure. However, a very poor result must not be ignored. You should seek the advice of a doctor or qualified psychologist. This may best be done by approaching the family doctor in the first place.

Mental retardation is seen by most psychiatrists as being a very distinct and separate type of mental abnormality from the neurotic or psychotic abnormalities, though of course there is some overlap, and neurotic and psychotic conditions do exist in retardates.

A fair view of the incidence of retardation is given by the following diagram. The curve shows the distribution of intelligence and retardation. On many grounds, this graph gives the most likely explanation of what is observed. This curve is based on the work of Binet. What it indicates is that the gaussian curve, which indicates the normal distribution of intelligence, is distorted at the lower tail by a hump that reflects the heavy incidence of severe disability caused either by accidental damage to the brain itself or by severe genetic abnormalities. In their *Handbook of*

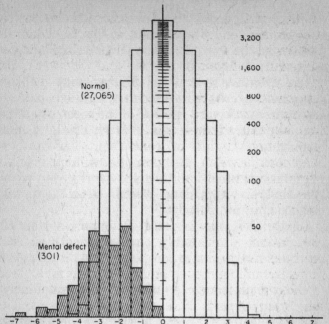

Abnormal Psychology, A. M. and A. D. B. Clarke say: 'If the reader expected to gain clear knowledge from experimental studies of the precise nature and extent of the retardates' deficiencies and the methods by which these can be ameliorated, he will have been disappointed. In almost every area in which the methods of experimental psychology have been applied, apparently conflicting results have been reported.'

We are, unfortunately, confined once again to the strategy of the best guess. On the whole, however, the Clarkes support the concept that there are two separate kinds of mental defects: those where there is some visible organic impairment and those where there is not. There seem to

115

be no clear behavioural differences between the two groups. They both seem to fit the general pattern at the low end of the normal distribution curve for intelligence.

The greatest success in dealing with mental retardation comes from a technique called *operant learning*. At the very low end of the spectrum, it is the only thing that seems to work at all. It has been found useful in controlling undesirable behaviour, such as head banging, window breaking, and bad toilet habits, and it works even with the severely retarded, where other training methods fail completely.

Operant learning is a straightforward system of reward and punishment, euphemistically called positive and negative reinforcement. The more immediate the response and the more it is related to the action, the more quickly and permanently the child responds.

The preferred method is to transfer the training from the actual to the symbolic. To begin with, for instance, the child is given a desirable reward for a success, accompanied by a smile and encouraging words. For a failure, it is given a mild slap or deprived of something, and the parent frowns and scolds. Eventually the reward and the slap can be eliminated as the training proceeds and the child is found to react to the praise or scolding.

Some severe abnormalities have visible genetic effects that can be seen by an examination of the body's cells. Mongolism (Down's syndrome) is caused by a small extra chromosome in the G group. Mongoloids have forty-seven instead of forty-six chromosomes. Mongolism, although determined at the moment of conception, does not seem to run in families but rather appears to be a kind of genetic accident. Many of these children used to die, but now the chance of survival is much better. Mongoloid children are frequently very easy to deal with and are often very much loved by their parents, who find looking after them quite rewarding.

Another very clearly noticeable genetic defect is phenylketonuria, which affects five per hundred thousand live births. It is caused by a single gene, and 25 per cent of the brothers and sisters of those who have the disease have it themselves. A high proportion, up to 10 per cent, of the parents of children with phenylketonuria are first cousins. The condition has a definite effect on the body chemistry, and the results on the mentality of the child depend on nutrition. If the condition is discovered at birth and a special diet started immediately, the average I.Q. of those children on the special diet is 89. But if the special diet is started after the seventy-second month, the average I.Q. is only 57.

Retardates tend to be outer directed, not inner directed as any bright, normal child would be – that is, in a problem situation, retardates look for cues and suggestions from the behaviour of other children around them, trying to see what solutions other children are using. They do this rather than trust their own judgment. This occurs, not because of the defect itself, but from a continuous experience of failure. The behaviour and learning failures of retardates thus tend to be self-reinforcing.

One wonders whether this explains the well known tractability and amiability of retardate children. Parents confronted with naughty, obstinate, and excessively self-willed (inner directed) children may find them irritating, but they will be happy to accept this as it bodes well for the final personality and ability of the child.

The lesson for the parent of a retarded child is that the level of problem setting should be very carefully adjusted to give the child an adequate ration of success so as to encourage it to trust its judgment up to a realistic level. It should be encouraged to learn its limitations and not stop short and overexaggerate them.

Severe retardation is usually caused by birth trauma such as anoxia. Anoxia occurs when the foetal brain is deprived of oxygen for a period sufficiently long for it to suffer permanent damage. Other causes of such retardation are certain infective diseases of the mother, such as German measles (rubella), syphilis, and toxoplasmosis.

It is the less severe forms of retardation which seem to have familial causes. In these cases, the near relatives of the affected child are often retarded themselves. In the investigation of such cases an incestuous relationship is often suspected. Unfortunately incest is more frequent among retarded people. Since the same genes in related individuals are deficient, the children produced are likely to be severely retarded.

Another group of retardates are those where the genetic instructions are normal but where the development of the brain is prevented by other faults of the system. Cretinism, for example, is usually caused by a thyroid deficiency. If observed early enough the deficiency can be corrected by injections and the child will develop more normally.

Failures of development can be caused by encephalitis and epilepsy. Although these diseases are not in themselves associated with mental defect, they can cause brain damage because children who have frequent fits suffer brain damage from anoxia. Maternal malnutrition and deprivation of stimulus to the baby can also reduce mental development.

There are also certain poisons which can hinder full development. One of these, which is being more noticed recently, is lead poisoning. Recently, too much alcohol during pregnancy has been suspected.

The Autistic Child

One of the conditions of mental testing is that the child or person tested is motivated to succeed. The subject must respond, or the results are meaningless.

Among those who will be labelled untestable on the normal I.Q. test is a class of children who are variously called autistic or non-communicating children. Like many terms employed in psychology and psychiatry, the term *autistic* seems to have a number of differing meanings and probably covers a number of different functional conditions. Among the parents who are perplexed about their children and who turn to this book for guidance, there may be some who have an autistic child. If the description of the symptoms seems to fit their child, they should apply immediately for skilled advice.

The condition was first diagnosed as a syndrome, or collection of typical symptoms, by Dr Leo Kanner, of Johns Hopkins University in Baltimore, Maryland. Dr Kanner says:

119

Autistic children are those who show extreme aloneness from the beginning of life, and an anxiously obsessive desire for the preservation of sameness. ... The common denominator in all these patients is a disability to relate themselves in the ordinary way to people and situations from the beginning of life. ... The case histories indicate invariably the presence from the start of extreme autistic aloneness which, wherever possible, shuts out anything that comes to the child from the outside. ... They reject reality, tend to brood, and become obsessed with small repetitious activities.

Translated into lay terms, the above quotation means that there are nine points to watch for. Almost all normal children will exhibit *some* of these characteristics *some* of the time. A parent should be concerned only if the child shows *excessive* tendencies in a number of these directions. Autistic children show:

1. Impaired emotional relationships with people and abnormal behaviour toward them such as 'treating them like tools or objects. They also may show a long lasting difficulty in playing with other children.
2. Unawareness of self beyond the usual age; the child may hurt itself by head banging or other types of aggression toward the self
3. Posturing or undue exploration and scrutiny of parts of the body
4. Undue and unduly prolonged attention to articles without regard to how they are used
5. A determined and prolonged resistance to

any change in the surroundings and continued attempts to maintain or restore what they are used to – the children seem to be attracted to complete monotony

6. Exaggerated or diminished response to normal happenings – for example, refusing to see or listen, or being insensitive to pain and temperature; excessive and illogical anxiety beyond what would normally be expected in a child; strange fears and phobias of harmless objects

7. Failure to learn to talk or very much delayed talking; strange mannerisms in speech that seem to have no meaning

8. Strange postures and mannerisms, rocking or spinning, 'freezing' in one attitude

9. Odd mixtures of apparent retardedness with occasional normal or near normal interludes.

Those who work with autistic children feel that it is not the intelligence of the child that is in doubt. They feel there is a fundamental defect that prevents the child from forming proper relationships and responding normally to what happens.

There is no advice that a layman can sensibly give a parent with an autistic child except to seek professional help as quickly as possible.

Dyslexia

Dyslexia, or *word blindness*, is the condition of a child who is otherwise of normal intelligence. The child is supposed to have a special disability that prevents it from learning to read. However, informed opinion appears to be crystallizing around the position that this is not an entirely accurate concept. Several careful studies in fair sized sample populations seem to give credible evidence that there is no real distinction between dyslexia and normal retardation or backwardness.

Brain Damage

Cerebral palsy, spasticity, and epilepsy are, it is generally agreed, usually due to brain damage – often brain damage that occurred during birth. Difficult births and breech births are well known to involve an increased risk.

Cerebral palsy, a disorder of movement and posture, may be associated with epilepsy, retardation, and disturbances of personality and emotion. It might show itself in simple cases as clumsiness in movement – the failure to use one of the senses effectively. The child may be able to see, but it cannot recognize objects by sight though it can do so by touch. Parents should seek medical advice if they have the slightest suspicion that the description fits their child.

What are the chances that your child will be retarded? In 1951 in the United Kingdom, it was estimated that a little over 1 per cent of the population exhibited some degree of mental subnormality. In general, the upper limit of I.Q. for retardates has been arbitrarily set at 70, and about 75 per cent of children classified as retarded are usually between I.Q. 50 and 70, 20 per cent are between I.Q. 20 and 50, and 5 per cent are more or less untestable at I.Q. 20 or below.

If the score you obtain for your child gives an I.Q. of below 70, it would be wise, before you commit yourself to a final judgment, to wait a few weeks until the child has forgotten the test and try again under the most favourable circumstances you can contrive. If the second result confirms the first one, then you should seek professional advice.

Reducing the Risk of Having a Subnormal Child?

Far too little is known about the causation of the various types of mental subnormality, and almost all authorities agree that much more research needs to be done. Nonetheless, a considerable body of information has been accumulated, and there are some precautions that can, at least to some extent, minimize the risk for any parent.

Generally speaking, the evidence points to three types of mental subnormality. In the first type, the causation is largely inborn, and this can be divided into two classes. One class already mentioned involves a gross chromosomal defect, such as phenylketonuria or Down's syndrome (Mongolism), where there is some apparent and visible defect in the body of one or both parents that can be detected by examination of body cells. Particularly if there is any incidence of heritable mental abnormality in the family would it be wise for a couple to consult genetic counsellors about the risk before they are married or, at any rate, before they have children of their own. One such specific risk that is genetic is rhesus incompatibility, or the *RH factor*, in which the blood types of the mother and father are incompatible and cause the mother to be sensitized after the first birth so that later babies are at risk.

123

The second type of genetic defect is much more difficult to deal with; it is a defect due to the normal variations in human ability. The first type is due to one simple defect in a chromosome; the second is probably multifactorial. The particular mix of genes that the child happens to have is an unfortunate one. There seems to be little that can be done about this problem. We can only say that the risk of having a seriously subnormal child is lower for those people whose mental ability is above normal but even for them it is not eliminated. Generally speaking, each generation will tend to have children who are nearer to the average than they are, both upward and downward.

The third type of mental subnormality results from the damage that the child might sustain either while it is in the womb or at birth. Forceps deliveries sometimes cause brain damage that may lead to mental subnormality. An imperfect diet during pregnancy may cause problems, but this risk has been exaggerated and it is probably not great. A much more serious source of risk is medication, particularly self-medication. The Thalidomide children represent only an extreme example of the risks associated with the taking of drugs, which may not always be realized even by the doctors who prescribe them. Self-medication is obviously more dangerous than drugs prescribed by doctors. On the whole, we may say that the fewer drugs of any kind a woman takes during pregnancy, the lower the risk of abnormalities. Shortage or excess of oxygen given during childbirth can cause problems, and an excess of oxygen in particular has been shown to cause a certain type of blindness. Age is another factor since it is well known that the incidence of Down's syndrome increases with the mother's age. Bearing children after thirty-five or so may be risky. In some cases, such as hydrocephalus (water on the brain) and spina bifida, there is a very clear mixture of heredity and environmental factors.

If there seems to be a predisposition in the mother that is probably inherited, it can be reduced or increased according to her diet at the time of pregnancy. If you are aware of any of these diseases in your ancestry, you would be wise to consult a specialist.

CHAPTER EIGHT

Does Intelligence Run in Families?

Early ideas about the inheritance of human qualities are confused. Being of good *stock* or of good *blood* once clearly had the implication of genetic superiority – an idea probably taken from stock breeding. But the meaning of *good breeding* was an odd mixture of inheritance and good manners – that is, the behaviour usual in the upper classes. The idea that there was some special quality attached to royal or aristocratic *noble* families was universally accepted. This quality was a mixture of nature and nurture. There was no preciseness as to the properties involved. Characteristics such as *nobility* or *baseness* were deemed to be inheritable, but they seemed to relate more to martial qualities, courage, and aggressiveness than to intelligence.

With the major social changes that have occurred over the past two hundred years, the idea that one particular social class has a monopoly of desirable human qualities has been rejected. It was a simple, observable fact that such qualities could be found in any social class. The rising middle class slowly and cautiously rejected the assumption of hereditary superiority held by their traditional rulers. The process is not yet complete, and there remains a residual respect for aristocrats, who still enjoy a reputation (or at least a *cachet*) that has little justification. The middle classes have mimicked the traditional upper class inbreeding and now have their own unstated claim to genetic superiority. But the set of ideas that underlies the policies in most countries today is opposed to the notion of genetic superiority on any level.

The argument that intelligence has little to do with parentage has become so vehement that we might start by looking at something very obvious. The intelligence of humanity as a species is clearly and undeniably genetic. No matter what environments we rear animals in, we do not get intelligence remotely comparable to that of normal human beings. The most extreme environmentalist accepts that the differences in intelligence between humans and other animals are largely genetic. What is denied is that the differences *between* human beings are accounted for by genetics. Unlike all other human attributes, such as height, weight, skin, and hair colour (which vary for genetic reasons between individuals), intelligence, it is believed, is the same for everyone at birth. For anyone who has ever actually met children or tried to educate them, this is difficult to believe.

First, let us give something of the evidence advanced to support the hereditarian view.

Those who emphasize the genetic influence concede very considerable influence to environment. The proportion varies. The most popular way of putting it is that about 20 per cent of the variation in general mental ability among people is accounted for by environmental factors. One of the lowest estimates was given by Sir Cyril Burt, who attributed only 7 per cent of the variation to environmental sources. Other estimates make the environmental contribution as high as 50 per cent. The remaining portion of the variation, Sir Cyril Burt and other hereditarians say, is inherited from parents. We might reasonably ask how such wide variations in estimates occur.

We must accept that we are looking at a problem of extraordinary difficulty. We cannot experiment genetically with human beings. So any evidence must come from what actually happens without experimental interference.

Psychology has taken two different approaches, and the two methodologies tend to drive scientists to different conclusions. The current behaviourist school of psychology arose from the work of Pavlov and Watson. It looks upon the individual animal or human as a 'black box' and reaches its conclusions from an examination of the information input and the behavioural output. The hidden assumption is that each subject is an identical entity.

We cannot erect a whole behavioural science about every individual, and it is therefore convenient to look for and generalize from evidence that is as unaffected as possible by individual differences. It is the whole class *cat* or *dog* or *human* that is being examined and the variations within that class that obstruct advance. Most schools of sociology tend to ignore individual differences and regard man as the standard atom of the system.

The opposite approach, psychometry, which is the psychology of individual differences, concerns itself with the problem of classifying the animal investigated into subgroups and then predicting behavioural variations from these classifications.

Obviously, both approaches are valuable, and both can lead to predictive generalizations. Nonetheless, it is not surprising if there are some very sharp differences in their conclusions. The differences were built in at the foundation of the two disciplines.

Trying for an overview, we must first concede that the similarities between people are more important and more marked than the differences. We are almost all born with one head, two eyes, two ears, ten fingers, and a vast number of other points of similarity. But this does not mean that the differences are unimportant or that an examination of the differences would be unproductive, immoral, or invalid. As long as we live in a complex industrial society where people are fitted into many different roles, some of which are extremely exacting and specific, we need to understand the differences that make some of us more effective at some tasks. As long as mankind exhibits a wide variety of behavioural inadequacies and disorders, we need to try to understand the differences between those in trouble and those with normal behaviour so that effective help can be provided at each level of development.

A widespread error in this field is the concept of single causation. Great progress was made in the world of the physical sciences by controlling all variables except one and thus isolating each separate effect upon an otherwise stable system. With simple physical systems, this works well enough; but in complex systems, it often happens that there is an interaction among variables that makes it inappropriate and misleading to look at them in isolation.

Each human being is born with a potential to learn and with some individual differences. The amount that is learned after birth is so vast, compared with the tiny array of inborn behaviour, that it is not surprising that a good deal of emphasis is given to the environment. What is immediately apparent is the susceptibility of new-born babies to their environment. The complicated behaviour patterns, movements, and elaborate skills are developed during a lifetime. But the question some psychologists ask, and try to answer, is 'To what extent is the development of a child an unfolding of a potential, innate pattern, and to what extent is its progress changed by the child's experience?'

The environmentalists* tend to answer this question with other questions: 'Why do you want to know?' 'How can you possibly disentangle the two factors?' The psychologists answer by a serious attempt to assess differences. How can we disentangle the two threads – the initial potential and the actual development? There are several ways.

Twin Studies

About one in eighty-seven births is of twins. Twins are of two types: fraternal (from two eggs) and identical (from one egg). Fraternal twins have the same relation as two brothers or two sisters; they come from two separate ova fertilized by two

*The word 'environmentalist' is used here to describe those who believe that most of the difference in intelligence between people is accounted for by their environment or upbringing.

separate sperms. Identical twins come from the splitting of a single ovum fertilized by a single sperm. They are, from a genetic point of view, very nearly identical.

Anyone who has met identical twins is aware how close the resemblance is. They offer us a good clue as to the amount of variation that can be expected due to environment and due to heredity. During the early years of the century, it was common to split up pairs of twins because the parents were unable economically to cope with both.

A great similarity between the intelligence assessments of identical twins had long been known, but it had always been argued by the environmentalists that if they were brought up together their environmental circumstances would also be very similar.

Sir Cyril Burt was the first to use separated twins as a means of answering this argument. Since then, completely independent studies have been done, and large numbers of separated identical twins have been discovered. The result of this mass of work in many places by many researchers has always shown the same tendency. It has shown, first, that one-egg twins reared apart resemble one another very much more in intelligence than two-egg twins reared together. They have also shown that one-egg twins brought up together show even more resemblance in intelligence quotient. Thus, it is conclusively shown that there is both a genetic and environmental influence on the manifest I.Q. and that the effect of heredity is more important.

Erlenmeyer-Kimling and Jarvik in 1963 summarized the evidence of fifty-two genetic studies from eight countries, spanning half a century of time, and employing a wide variety of tests and subjects. They found the following data:

TABLE 4

	Correlation	Coefficients
Group	Reared Apart	Reared Together
Unrelated persons	−0·01	0·23
Foster parents and their children		0·20
Parents and their children		0·5
Brothers and sisters	0·4	0·49
Fraternal twins		0·53
Identical twins	0·75	0·87

The most significant thing in this table is that completely unrelated persons reared together show a very low resemblance in intelligence (0·25), whereas twins, who have exactly the same genetic makeup, reared apart show a very high resemblance in I.Q. (0·75).

These studies show conclusively that the genetic effect is a very strong one and that certainly the environmental influence is also important.

It should also be noted that the brother and sister, fraternal twins, and parent and child correlation coefficients are all around the 0·5 level, which would be predicted by a genetic explanation. It is very difficult to think of an explanation on environmental grounds alone compatible with figures like these.

One refuge for the environmentalists has been to say that similarities between twins reared apart can be accounted for by the fact that the very early environment has an extremely strong influence so that the similarity of the twins is established even before the separation. Against this, it has been shown in one study that the age of parting makes no difference. In fact, another study showed that twins separated earlier show *more* similarity instead of less.

In a series of interesting investigations with identical and fraternal twins reared together and apart, it was shown that the correlation between the pairs in educational attainment was much more closely related to their environment than was their intelligence measure.

A point that is often missed in discussions about the relative contribution of heredity and environment to mental differences is that any statement that may be made can only be related to a given population at a given time.

The fact that the many studies tend to agree is an indication that the range of environmental variation in those populations must have been approximately the same.

A way to illustrate this point is to think of two extreme situations. Imagine a population which consists entirely of a clone of identical individuals. Every member of the population has exactly the same genetic constitution and therefore within such a clone all the variability in manifest intelligence is due to environmental differences and nothing to heredity.

At the other extreme we may imagine a society which is genetically random but in which every child is brought up in exactly the same way. Here the contribution of the environment to manifest differences in intelligence would be near zero and the contribution of heredity would be 100 per cent.

So there is nothing absolute or permanent about the proportion 80 to 20 per cent. In advanced countries there has been a considerable reduction in the differences between the advantaged and disadvantaged population since the original studies were made. It seems likely that if these studies were repeated today the lowered variability in the environment would be reflected by an increase in the contribution of heredity to manifest differences.

Inheritance of Mental Defect

There is evidence for the inheritability of mental defects. In 1952, experiments made it clear that there appeared to be two kinds of variation in mentally retarded children and that the normal distribution, which had been assumed since 1912, was in fact distorted at the lower end by another group, specifically those with gross mental defects. This group seemed to be a population within a population, and in some ways it was preferable to look at it separately.

Approximately a quarter of the children admitted to institutions as severely subnormal have visible chromosome aberrations such as Mongolism, and as many as 45 per cent have fairly clear genetic factors – for instance, a family history of retardation, which would appear to predispose the children to their infirmity.

The evidence of mental defects in the relatives

of defective children is interesting and in some ways contradictory. The most severely handicapped children, those with an I.Q. range from 35 to 60, have brothers and sisters who appear to be fairly normal. These severely handicapped children's disabilities seem to be serious and are probably rare genetic effects. They are very often visible, as mentioned above, as a major defect that can be seen in the body or the chromosomes. The brothers and sisters of the less severely disabled group, those from a 60 I.Q. upward, tend to be diagnosed as definitely retarded. Usually the I.Q. of this group of siblings tends to be about halfway between the average of the defective group and the average of all children. This could be accounted for if we assume that the higher grade defectives or retardates are accounted for by the normal inherited variations between individuals (they are simply on the lower tail of the distribution curve), whereas the extremely low grade defectives result from, as suggested, a more dramatic and rarer gross genetic defect, which is unlikely to affect two members of one family. A gross genetic defect cannot be passed on to the next generation because almost all those affected are, in fact, sterile. These defects can only happen by a rare unhappy genetic accident, a mutation, or a unique combination of genes.

Parent Type and Subnormal Children

The families of a group of subnormal children were examined with these results:

Parents	Siblings of Subject Who Are Subnormal (%)
Both subnormal	42·1
One subnormal	19·9
Both normal, with subnormal uncles or aunts	12·9
All relatives normal	5·7

It seems established beyond any reasonable doubt that the causes of high or low intelligence in children are a mixture of both environment and heredity; and it does appear equally certain that heredity plays a more important part.

Some people ask: If intelligence is largely genetic, is the general level of intelligence of the community rising or falling? Some geneticists in the past have had serious fears that there may be a lowering of the general level of intelligence because of the observed trend of differential fertility of different social groups and the difference in intelligence in those groups. It was observed that the families of parents with lower intelligence test scores were on the average larger than those of parents with higher scores. However, later studies indicate that this effect is outbalanced by a reduced fertility at the lower end of the test score spectrum. It is rare for severely retarded persons to have children or to marry at all. In addition, recently there has been a marked increase in fertility at the top end of the intelligence score scale in some countries. All in all, observers seem to be satisfied that there is at least a rise, not a fall, in the general level of intelligence.

The reader who would like to know more about the question of heredity and environment and their contribution to the variations in intelligence test scores can get a very good account from Professor Eysenck's book *The Inequality of Man*. In this book, the arguments pro and con are dealt with very carefully and systematically. Professor Eysenck points out that, whereas any conclusion in this field is open to some uncertainty, all the evidence there is is consistent with the hypothesis that about 20 per cent of the variability in I.Q. scores can be accounted for by environment and about 80 per cent must be attributed to heredity.

Professor Eysenck points out that the nature of the problem is misunderstood. Every characteristic of an animal is both genetic and environmental in origin; any argument can only be about the contribution of the different causes. The inborn, or genetic, characteristics will present a ceiling. The environment, or the way the child is brought up, determines how close to that ceiling the child can get. Eysenck goes on to say that in the past there has been uncertainty because it was difficult to determine the effect of the interaction between the inborn and environmental factors. Now that it is known to be both measurable and quite small, accurate estimates can be made. It turns out that the estimates of early researchers, notably Holzinger, Freeman, and Burt, were not far afield despite the fact that their methods were open to, and certainly received, much subsequent criticism. Recent work with more refined methods has produced figures very similar to these first estimates.

An important point that is often missed is that any error or uncertainty in the reliability of the tests themselves will automatically have the effect of reducing any estimate that may be made of the inheritability of intelligence. The uncertainty from the test instrument itself would tend to reduce the high correlations found between unrelated children reared together.

Any such unreliability would tend to diminish differences shown in the correlation coefficient. Despite this, in all investigations into one-egg twins reared together and apart, fraternal twins, and brothers and sisters reared together and apart, the correlation between the test scores of children adopted at birth and their natural parents, the correlation between the scores of children brought up in the same environment – as in orphanages – but of different parentage, and the correlation between the scores of children and foster parents tend to confirm the 80% contribution by heredity to mental differences. Every experiment, without exception, tends to confirm the general picture.

CHAPTER NINE

The Mental Resources of Humanity

What distinguishes the inanimate universe from living things is that the latter group tend to resist changes in their form and be stability seeking, or homeostatic. An essential element of any stability seeking system must be a means for obtaining, processing, and acting on information from the environment. Stability seeking entities, or 'morphostats,' whether they be organizations or organisms, tend to resist the universal disordering force in the universe – entropy – using coded and processed information to trigger counteracting or adaptive forces. All data processing systems are associated with living systems and all living systems have data processing capabilities. In simple terms, intelligence, what we are trying to measure in your child, is the data processing capability. There are few who would deny that the human brain is the best instrument for data processing that we know of in the universe, and so we can claim that the most human thing about human beings is their highly developed intelligence.

In the authors' opinion the advantages to humanity of the human being's very large and elaborate brain do not lie in the brain's effectiveness for the individual but in its service to the complicated organizations and societies that humans live in. Animals with brains inferior to human brains are quite capable of a solitary life or of life in small groups. The increased size of the human brain may have evolved so that human beings could live successfully in large complex, well organized, and stable groups.

It follows that smaller, simpler social groupings do not require as high a level of intelligence for their organization as do larger, more complicated ones like those that have appeared in the developed world in the last few hundred years.

Zipf and other researchers have shown that the liability to error and the complexity of an information network increase exponentially with size. We may expect, therefore, that as the separate living societies of the world coalesce into one worldwide society, the problems of communication and organization will become increasingly severe. Added to these problems are those presented by the accelerating growth of population in many lands. Few people would deny that toward the end of this century, mankind as a whole will be faced by problems that will require the most intensive application of that most human quality – intelligence.

The demand for human ability, intelligence, and talent will be great and increasing if all these problems are to be solved. The world of tomorrow, even more than the world of today, will need to find, motivate, educate, exploit, and use all the talent that is available to it in each generation.

We shall be unable to afford the enormous waste of talent that exists even in the developed world, much less the waste in the vast population that is living at subsistence level in the underdeveloped nations. The people in these countries, without access to proper education, books, and stimulation, spend their life at simple tasks that could be performed well by machines. Mankind is faced with two alternatives: either man will have to use his brain, collectively and individually, more effectively, or he will have to revert to an earlier, simpler style of life and reduce his numbers drastically.

If this latter road is taken, whether by choice or by incompetence and failure, the changes required are so severe and all-encompassing that the human inhabitants of this world can look forward only to several generations of calamity.

The only other viable alternative is for mankind to try to think and organize his way out of the problems that his very successes have created. The options are few. Our societies will have to find the right course if we are to avoid the many kinds of disaster that could overwhelm us.

Parents who want to realize a good future for their children and their children's children can best do this by making sure that their children fulfil their potential so that they can be of the most service to society. The parents whose problem and privilege it is to have a gifted child have an even more urgent task and duty because it is from these children that we must recruit those who lead the rest of us.

To be deflected by false egalitarians, an unthinking 'sense of fairness,' compensationitis, and the tides of uninstructed public opinion is to be the enemy of the people of tomorrow. And educators should stop trying to be social reformers and return to the task of helping children to acquire the academic skills they need to reap the harvest of our rich cultural heritage.

When we review the enormous range in human ability and behaviour from the moron or uncommunicating autistic child, on the one hand, to the brilliant, eagerly learning, able child on the other, it is difficult to understand how anyone can believe that benefits to the children and to society can be achieved by a monolithic undiscriminating system built on the hypothesis that all variations in humans are unimportant or largely culturally determined.

The idea that every man shall have equal rights – that all men are legally, morally, and socially equal – is an essential element of any humane society. But the extension of this idea – that all men are in reality equal, that there is a kind of international standard man to which we all conform – is one of the more extreme ideas of Rousseau. It is a comic idea, and it is comic that it is taken seriously. But the consequences of taking it seriously and of trying to formulate educational policy in its light are not comic, they are tragic. They constitute an abandonment of that essential ethic of Western society's success, the doctrine of 'the best man for the job.'

It is not the able people especially who will suffer from society's neglect; they can look after themselves in most circumstances and will, as always, do better than average under any system, no matter how much it may try to handicap them. It is the society as a whole that will be impoverished, as it is in areas of the world where nepotism, corruption, and ideological or religious purity, not ability, are the basis of selection and promotion.

The principal virtue of democracy is that it releases the talents of the people to contend in fair competition so that ability emerges where it can have the most influence. The defect of the system is that individual objectives are often merely private profit and personal advancement. What the world needs is a system that provides a viable programme of selection that would face with clear eyes the inequality of man and would make the best, compassionate, humane, and effective use of human mental resources. The subject would seem to be one that is worthy of a great deal more study than it has attracted so far.

We hope that eventually a climate of opinion will emerge that will make it possible to study the demand for, the supply of, the social motivation of, and the education and training of that most precious of human resources – intelligence.

Appendix 1

When you have got some indication of your child's percentile rating on intelligence from the tests in this book, you will obviously want to know what the vocational opportunities are for the various levels of mental ability.

The following table will give some guidance. The table was developed from data contained in *Performance Norms on Job Applicants*, Northfield, Illinois: by E. F. Wonderlic & Associates Inc., 1970.

It does not of course tell us the intelligence of people in jobs because it is not easy to get figures for these, but many applicants are subjected to intelligence tests and most have a reasonably good idea of their chances. These figures then give a rough guide.

For each group there are given a number of figures.

Firstly we give the average of all the applicants for jobs in that group. Taking the top group, Administrators, Engineers, Personnel Specialists and Medical Secretaries, all the applicants averaged the 83rd percentile. That is, they scored better than 83% of the population.

The second line gives the range or spread of the middle half of the applicants. In other words, if you ranked all the applicants for I.Q. and then cut off the top and bottom 25%, the cut off points would be the 'range of middle 50%'. In the case of the group mentioned this means that only a quarter of the applicants scored worse than 62% of the population and a quarter scored more than 94% of the population.

We must remember that this was only applicants. It is very likely that only those at the higher end of each range were the *successful* applicants.

*Approximate Intelligence Percentiles of Job Applicants**

Administrator	Average (median) 83rd percentile
Engineer	Range of middle 50% 62nd–94th percentile
Personnel Specialist	
Medical Secretary	

Department Head	Average (median) 79th percentile
General Manager	Range of middle 50% 57th–93rd percentile
Insurance Sales	
Representative	
Programmer	
Underwriter	

Claims Adjuster	Average (median) 75th percentile
Inspector	Range of middle 50% 53rd–91st percentile
Laboratory	
Technician	
Management Trainee	
Purchasing Agent	
Supervisor	

Accounting Clerk	Average (median) 70th percentile
Computer Operator	Range of middle 50% 48th–88th percentile
Sales Representative	

*Developed from data contained in *Performance Norms on Job Applicants*. Northfield, Illinois: E. F. Wonderlic & Associates, Inc., 1970.

Bookkeeper	Average (median) 62nd percentile
Cashier	Range of middle 50% 43rd–83rd percentile
Data Processing	
Clerk	
Draughtsman	
News Writer	
Stenographer	
Traffic Clerk	

Circulation Manager	Average (median) 57th percentile
Customer Service	Range of middle 50% 34th–79th percentile
Representative	
Electrician	
Foreman	
General Office	
Lineman	
Office Machine	
Operator	
Receptionist	
Technician	
Teller	

Apprentice, Shop	Average (median) 53rd percentile
Clerk	Range of middle 50% 26th–75th percentile
Clerk Typist	
Reservations Agent	
Typist	

Keypunch Operator	Average (median) 48th percentile
Messenger	Range of middle 50% 26th–71st percentile
Meter Reader	
Police Patrolman	
Skilled Trades	
Train Crew	
Personnel	

Bus/Truck Driver	Average (median) 43rd percentile
Machine Operator	Range of middle 50% 22nd–67th percentile
Mail Clerk	
Maintenance Worker	
Printing Pressman	
Utility Man	
Traffic Supervisor	

Food Service Worker	Average (median) 38th percentile
Helper, General	Range of middle 50% 16th–67th percentile
Mechanic's Helper	
Shipping Clerk	

File Clerk	Average (median) 34th percentile
Material Handler	Range of middle 50% 16th–62nd percentile
Telephone Operator	

Assembler	Average (median) 29th percentile
Factory Worker, General	Range of middle 50% 12th–57th percentile
Labourer	
Skilled Labour	
Unskilled Labour	

Custodian	Average (median) 24th percentile
Nurse's Aide	Range of middle 50% 10th–55th percentile
Packer	
Warehouseman	

Appendix 2

Organizations and what they can do for you.

The National Association for Gifted Children, 1 South Audley Street, London, WC2N 6HX, U.K.
  (Assistance with gifted children).

Headquarters, British Mensa Limited (and Mensa International Limited), Bond House, St John's Square, Wolverhampton, WV2 4HA, U.K.
  (Membership open to persons who score at the top 2% level in I.Q. tests. Supervised group tests in most areas).

The British Psychological Society, 18 Albemarle Street, London, W1, U.K.
  (Lists of qualified Psychologists).

The Independent Assessment and Research Centre Ltd, 57 Marylebone High Street, London, W1M 3AE, U.K.
  (Vocational guidance and tests).

The National Foundation for Educational Research, The Mere, Upton Park, Slough, Bucks, U.K.
  (Vocational guidance).

The National Society for Mentally Handicapped Children, Pembridge Hall, 17 Pembridge Square, London, W2, U.K.
  (Help for retarded children).

Index

And selected from the SPHERE
Childcare List

KINDERGARTEN IS TOO LATE

MASARU IBUKA

IS YOUR CHILD MISSING OUT?

Can a pre-school child learn foreign languages? Can he
or she be taught to play a musical instrument?

Masaru Ibuka is convinced that we waste the best years
of our children's lives – the years between nought and
three, when, he believes, a human being's creative and
learning potential is at its maximum.

This remarkable and revolutionary book presents a plan
for the transformation of our entire approach to bringing
up small children. It is based on the idea that small
children are totally learning-oriented – and cites cases of
normal two- and three-year olds being taught music and
foreign languages. Mr Masaru's ideas are already being
put into practice in Japan by the Early Development
Association – with remarkable results. For any caring
parent of a pre-school child, KINDERGARTEN IS
TOO LATE is essential – and fascinating reading.

0 7221 4872 0   CHILDCARE

95p

A selection of Bestsellers from Sphere Books